The Little WordPerfect Book

Skye Lininger

Peachpit Press
Berkeley, California

The Little WordPerfect Book
Skye Lininger

Peachpit Press
2414 Sixth Street
Berkeley, CA 94710
(510) 548-4393
(510) 548-5991 (fax)

First Edition published 1991

ISBN: 0-938151-50-9

0 9 8 7 6 5 4 3 2 1

Printed and bound in the United States

Dedication:

To my father, who is always pleased when friends ask him how long he's been writing computer books. (That's the risk you run when father and son share the same name.)

To Helen, whose praise of childhood brush strokes is still remembered with fondness and affection.

About the author:

Skye Lininger, a chiropractor, has long used word processors and desktop publishing as business communication tools. An acknowledged expert on WordPerfect, he has contributed to more than half a dozen best-selling books on the subject.

Dr. Lininger is a contributing editor to *Personal Publishing* and writes regularly for *Let's Live, The WordPerfectionist, Ventura Professional!* and other magazines.

Along with his wife, also a chiropractor, he publishes a monthly newsletter, *HealthNotes*, that is distributed nationally by natural foods stores.

Serving as vice president of sales for a nutritional supplement company, he uses WordPerfect to write product literature and articles about natural health products. Dr. Lininger also teaches at Western States Chiropractic College in Portland, Oregon; and lectures extensively on nutrition to health care professionals in the United States and England.

About this book:

The Little WordPerfect Book was written using WordPerfect 5.1. Text was transmitted electronically, using CompuServe mailboxes, to my editors for review and corrections.

The design was created using PageMaker 4.01 on the Macintosh. Publication files were transmitted via CompuServe between the author and designer for review and modifications.

Sample printouts were either faxed or sent via Federal Express for review and approval.

The book was composed with PageMaker on a Macintosh IIcx and proofed using an Apple LaserWriter Plus PostScript printer. Fonts used were ITC Century Light and Bold, ITC Kabel, Franklin Gothic Heavy, and Zapf Dingbats–all from Adobe Systems.

Final output was from a Linotronic typesetter.

Acknowledgments:

No book is the work of a single person; and books for PeachPit Press involve a particularly enjoyable and energetic blend of collaborative efforts.

Thanks to Ted Nace for the opportunity to turn a brief proposal at a panel discussion into a book for a unique publisher. I especially appreciated the opportunity to put my desktop publishing knowledge to work producing a book from beginning to end.

Thanks to Moses Wine, a long-time friend whose talent as the developmental and technical editor for this book kept it focused, coherent, and accurate.

Thanks to Lisa Hunt Tally, who combined an intimate knowledge of WordPerfect with an energetic and skillful editing ability.

Thanks also to my wife, Jane (who was a great help with layout), and daughters Cory and Ciel. We all now know that designing a book takes at least as long as the writing.

Thanks to the WordPerfect Corporation for such great software and helpful personnel.

Special thanks and gratitude to the award-winning designer of this book, Lawrence Miller, president of the Atlanta-based Plato Picasso Midas Miller strategic design firm.

Larry served as both art director and designer. The art director function focused on the market the book was intended for. The concept was simplicity. Every effort went into making pages inviting to the eye–easy to read, neat, orderly–so each reader could navigate through the book with optimum comfort. He took care to make certain simplicity did not turn into dullness.

After being satisfied the design goals had been met, Larry functioned more as a pure designer, making the book artistically satisfying by adjusting weights, sizes, and positions–taking care none of this intruded on the original concept.

It was a pleasure working with Larry. He was professional, fastidious, willing to follow the design process from beginning to end. In many ways this book is as much his as it is mine.

Table of Contents

Chapter 1: Introducing WordPerfect

The *Little WordPerfect Book* is for the newcomer to computers or the newcomer to WordPerfect. The book is simple and straightforward, written in plain English for the non-computer person. You might consider this the "essential" WordPerfect book—one that leaves out what is unessential to performing most of your daily word processing tasks.

With this book, you'll learn fundamental WordPerfect skills so that within a reasonable time you'll know how to write letters and brief reports. For many of you, this book will be all you'll ever need.

If you've struggled with learning WordPerfect, or if you've ever sat down to type a letter and didn't know how to begin, or if you've been intimidated by

What is WordPerfect? Is it hard to use?

This book helps you over the fear hurdle.

In a short time, you're up and running—creating your own letters and reports.

the complexity of a word processor then this book is for you!

You're the person who has neither the time for nor the interest in mastering every complicated nuance of WordPerfect. You just want to get some work done, and you want to get it done now. You don't want to read through a 900-page book or browse the 1,000-page manual that comes with the program. You want to learn what's necessary and leave the details to the computer wizards. This book is for:

Who needs WordPerfect? Read over this list. You may find yourself described.

✻ **Secretaries or temporary workers** who are new to word processing or to WordPerfect and want to become productive quickly

✻ **Executives** without time to learn all WordPerfect's features but who want to write their own letters or reports

✻ **Entrepreneurs** in new businesses who don't have the staff or time but who need to be able to write letters and reports

✻ **People working out of a home office** who need WordPerfect for letters and reports to customers and associates

✻ **Students** who are new to WordPerfect and who need to write compositions and reports for school

✻ **Managers** proficient with WordPerfect, but who need a beginner's book for teaching the occasional or new user

What is a word processor?

The first question a newcomer to computers often asks is, "What is a word processor, anyway?" A word processor, such as WordPerfect, is a type of computer software designed to produce textual documents. Word processors have replaced typewriters in most offices. However, word processors are different from typewriters in a number of ways.

With a typewriter, each time you press a key, something happens on the paper. When you press the T key, for example, the character *T* is printed on the page. With a word processor, you can type a complete document, such as a letter, without printing anything. Only when you are satisfied with the letter do you print it all out at once.

Because a typewriter prints a character onto the page each time you press a key, correcting mistakes is tedious. Even the new electronic typewriters that can "erase" entire paragraphs take time and make the paper look messy.

With a word processor, you can make all the corrections before anything is printed. This capability makes correcting your document easier and less time-consuming.

In addition, with a typewriter, if you need to make a change somewhere on the page, you must physically move the paper to a new position. Doing so can cause the letters in a word to misalign. With a word processor, you can move the insertion point (called the *cursor*) anywhere you want in the document—and the letters always line up correctly.

Because a word processor can do everything a typewriter can do, but can do the work faster and with less effort, it's easy to see why almost everyone who has to write letters or reports prefers to use a word processor.

What is a word processor, anyway?

How is it like–and how is it different–from a typewriter?

1|4 Why this book was written

This is a basic book for beginners. It covers only the essentials so you can quickly learn how to write letters and reports.

You have chosen (or are thinking of choosing) WordPerfect because you have heard that it's the best word processor on the market. (This is true, by the way.) Like many professional tools, however, WordPerfect can be extremely intimidating, and it can take time to learn how to use.

Adding to the intimidation is a 1,000-page manual. I've been using WordPerfect ever since I got my first PC and have written or contributed to eight books about WordPerfect, none shorter than 500 pages! In looking over the bookstore shelves, I discovered that there were few (if any) books with the primary goal of teaching a beginner how to write a letter or short report in WordPerfect.

This book teaches basic WordPerfect skills

In combining a tutorial approach with a task orientation, this book differs from the massive manual or big WordPerfect books that cover all aspects of the program. It is not like the small quick-reference books that briefly explain the features of WordPerfect but are really refresher books for experts. And although there are other tutorial books for new users, this book's focus on common office skills required in your job or business sets it apart.

After writing about WordPerfect for many years, I've come to realize that many people don't want (or need) to become experts or computer "fanatics." They just want to know what is necessary for basic office work. Unfortunately, the way Word-Perfect is often taught can make the work harder instead of easier. Because WordPerfect is a complex program capable of churning out a sophisticated document, using it to write a letter can be daunting. This book focuses on the things you need to know to write a letter, streamlining the learning process.

Imagine that you have been given a performance sports car to use for driving to the local market for a loaf of bread. Although a sports car will certainly get you there, you won't use even a tenth of its capabilities. For example, you aren't likely to drive 200 miles an hour, you probably won't need to adjust the climate control, and you probably won't use the power-assisted steering to handle mountain curves. Not only that, but for a simple drive to the store, you won't even need to know what that dial over there means or what happens when you push that button.

WordPerfect is like the sports car. You may "only" need to write a letter even though Word-Perfect has more tools that it can place at your disposal. However, for basic letter or report writing, you not only won't use those capabilities, you don't even need to know about them. What you want and need to know are the fundamentals, and you want to learn them quickly and with the least confusion possible.

This book is logically organized

If you get to the intermediate or expert stage and want to learn about WordPerfect's advanced features, plenty of books can help you. In fact, because the WordPerfect books and manual don't know what you want to learn, they cover everything. (Even if you don't want to know about a particular feature, you still have to wade past the explanation of it to learn how to do things you *will* need to know.)

This book focuses on a particular need I've uncovered in teaching people about WordPerfect. Although you can learn how to write a letter or report with WordPerfect by reading the manual, that approach is not the quickest method. This book was written with simple jobs in mind and is organized logically in the order you need for doing those jobs. If you read and follow the examples in this book, by the time you finish it you will be able to write a letter or simple report in WordPerfect.

When you master this book, you will be ready for the manual or one of the many excellent WordPerfect books geared toward intermediate or advanced users. You may well find, however, that the things you learn in this book will be all you'll ever need to perform your word processing tasks.

Notes

Don't be afraid to write in the margins or in these special places provided for Notes.

Jot down your discoveries so you don't forget them.

Remember, it's okay to write in this book–after all it's just another tool!

How to use this book

The *Little WordPerfect Book* folds flat so that it will stay open while you're using your computer. If you do the exercises in the book, you'll learn more and retain the information better than if you just read the book and try to remember the concepts. Jot reminders in the margins and "Notes" area.

Each page builds on the next, so it is better to begin at the beginning instead of jumping into the middle somewhere. Each chapter is designed so that it won't take too long to read. Within a reasonable amount of time, you will know enough to be able to write letters in WordPerfect.

To make information easier to find, each major topic in a chapter begins on its own page. The heading will tell you what concept is being covered. In addition, many pages have an illustration. Usually the illustration will match what you are seeing on your own computer screen.

This book folds flat so it will stay open next to your computer.

Don't just read the examples, practice them.

What version of WordPerfect should you use?

WordPerfect regularly improves its software.

Be sure you are using the latest version.

This book is based on WordPerfect version 5.1. If you have an earlier version of WordPerfect, you should consider upgrading to the latest edition. To upgrade to 5.1, call WordPerfect at (800) 321-4566, with your WordPerfect license number ready. The upgrade costs $89, which you can pay with a credit card.

It is possible but not recommended to use this book with the software program LetterPerfect (a scaled-down version of WordPerfect), but some of the features described in this book aren't available in LetterPerfect.

It would be difficult, but not impossible, to use this book with WordPerfect 5.0. Some of the menu choices are different, and you won't be able to use a mouse or the pull-down menus. In addition, some newer features (such as tables) aren't included in version 5.0.

Don't try to use this book with WordPerfect 4.2. Version 4.2 is quite different from WordPerfect 5.0 and 5.1. Many of the changes from 4.2 to 5.0 or 5.1 make WordPerfect easier to learn and use, giving you an additional reason to upgrade.

Chapter 2: Beginning WordPerfect

This chapter teaches you some basics about WordPerfect. Every software program has its own idiosyncrasies–its own way of doing things. Most of the ways WordPerfect does things are intuitive and make a great deal of sense.

In this chapter you will learn:

✳ How to install WordPerfect (if it's not already installed)

✳ How to start WordPerfect

✳ How to quit WordPerfect

✳ What a "clean screen" is

✳ How a computer keyboard differs from a typewriter keyboard

✳ What a menu is and how you use one

By the time you've finished this chapter, you'll know about menus and how they work with WordPerfect.

2|10

✱ How to use WordPerfect's Help system
✱ What a hidden code is
✱ What a default setting is

Notes

_____

_____

_____

_____

_____

_____

_____

_____

_____

_____

_____

_____

_____

Reviewing some computer terms

Like anything new, computers come with their own language. One of the trickiest things to understand when you use a computer is the terminology. Most of the following words qualify as computer jargon, but because they appear so often in manuals for software, some definitions will be useful.

✻ Program or software. A program, also called software, is a list of instructions written in a computer language that lets you tell a computer what you want it to do. For example, WordPerfect is a program that lets you do word processing. Lotus 1-2-3 is a program that lets you manipulate numbers.

✻ Data, files, or documents. A program creates, edits, or works with data, which it stores in files. In WordPerfect, the data created might be a letter or report. WordPerfect calls these files "documents."

✻ Random-access memory (RAM) or computer memory. Your computer comes with a certain amount of RAM. Most systems sold today have at least 640K of memory. ("K" stands for "kilobytes" and is a unit of measure designating the size of a program or file.) Each program you have requires memory to run in. When you quit one program, the memory is freed up for another program to use. The program remains unchanged in memory, which is where the WordPerfect document is created and edited. Because RAM "remembers" only when there is power going to it, every so often you need to tell WordPerfect to "save" the document by copying it to disk.

Everything you learn comes with a new vocabulary.

This glossary of terms will help you in the world of word processing.

Disks can "remember" even when the power is turned off. If your document has not been saved to disk and your computer loses power, you may lose some or all of your work.

✳ **Hard drive or hard disk.** A hard disk is a large storage device that can hold programs and data. Its size is usually measured in "megabytes" (MB). Most computers these days have hard drives built in. You can copy programs and documents from floppy disks to the hard drive. Hard drives are much faster than floppy drives. Most users of WordPerfect have hard drives.

✳ **Floppy drive or floppy disk.** A floppy disk is a small storage device that is used primarily to transfer programs and data to your hard drive. Systems that don't have hard drives have to use floppy drives for running programs and storing documents. Because of the limited storage and slow speed of floppy drives, WordPerfect works much more efficiently on a hard drive system. Because of these advantages, if your system has only floppy drives, start saving up for a hard drive.

✳ **Saving files or documents.** As mentioned earlier, when you first create a document in WordPerfect, it exists only in RAM. Until you save the document to your hard or floppy disk drive, if you quit WordPerfect or turn off your computer, the document will be lost. Saving documents is discussed in Chapter 3.

Understanding disk drives

If WordPerfect is already installed on your computer, you can skip over this section.

To run WordPerfect quickly and efficiently (that is, without having to change floppy disks to perform different functions), you need a computer with a hard drive. You can run WordPerfect without a hard drive, but you will need to swap disks for certain WordPerfect functions. The only requirement for using the floppy disk drives is that your computer must be equipped with the higher-capacity disk drives (either a 1.2M 5 1/4-inch or a 3 1/2-inch drive).

If your computer has limited disk storage, you might want to consider using the scaled-down version of WordPerfect called LetterPerfect. LetterPerfect requires less disk space than WordPerfect.

If you aren't sure what kind of disk drives your computer has, and you need to know, try looking at the documents that came with your computer. If your computer doesn't have any documentation, or if you can't figure out the documentation (not an uncommon occurrence), you can call one of three sources:

✻ A friend, co-worker, or relative who is knowledgeable about computers. Such people are rare treasures, and you should be nice to them because they can often help you out of electronic jams.

✻ The person who sold you the computer. Sometimes this person will know something about the computer, but don't count on it.

You can run WordPerfect either from your hard disk or floppy disk drive.

The program will operate faster running from a hard disk drive.

Which do you have?

✻ **A WordPerfect technical support person.** WordPerfect has a toll-free phone line that is open from 7 a.m. to 6 p.m. (MST). The person at WordPerfect can help you figure out your computer equipment and assist you in installing the program. The WordPerfect toll-free number is (800) 533-9605. This toll-free support number is a major reason why WordPerfect has such an excellent reputation–so don't hesitate to use this service.

If you're a night person and need help between 6 p.m. and 7 a.m., you can call WordPerfect at (801) 222-9010.

Notes

Installing WordPerfect

If WordPerfect is already installed, or if it is someone else's job to install software onto your computer, you can skip over this section.

If you need to install WordPerfect, make certain that your computer is running and that the DOS prompt (usually C> or C:\>) is on-screen. Then follow these steps:

1. Insert the Install/Learn/Utilities 1 disk into the floppy disk drive. (You can use either the regular 5 1/4-inch disks or the smaller 3 1/2-inch disks, depending on your system and what size disks came with your copy of WordPerfect.)

2. If you have put the disk into the top drive (usually drive A), type *A:* and press Enter. If you have put the disk into the bottom drive (usually drive B), type *B:* and press Enter.

3. Type *Install* and press Enter.

4. Follow the instructions as they are presented on the screen. You can install WordPerfect either to your hard disk (recommended) or to floppy disks (not recommended, but possible). The least complicated installation is the "Basic" one.

The reason installation to floppy disks is not recommended is that using floppy disks is much slower than using a hard disk. Also, because WordPerfect is a large program, many floppy disks are required, and you may find yourself swapping disks in and out when you use WordPerfect.

WordPerfect's "Install" program makes installation straightforward.

Starting WordPerfect

If WordPerfect is installed on your computer's hard drive, you can start the program by performing the following steps, after making certain that your computer is on and that the DOS prompt (usually C> or C:\>) is displayed:

1. Change to the directory that WordPerfect is in (usually C:\WP51). Type *CD \WP51* and press Enter.

2. Type *WP* and press Enter.

If WordPerfect is installed on floppy disks, and you have two floppy drives, you can start the program by performing the following steps:

1. Insert the WordPerfect 1 disk into drive A. Insert a blank, formatted disk (for storing your letters and reports) into drive B.

2. Type *B:* and press Enter.

3. Type *A:WP* and press Enter.

4. In response to the prompt, replace the WordPerfect 1 disk in drive A with the WordPerfect 2 disk.

If WordPerfect is installed on floppy disks, and you have one floppy drive, you can start the program by performing the following steps:

1. Insert the WordPerfect 1 disk into disk drive A.

2. Type *A:* and press Enter.

3. Type *WP* and press Enter.

4. In response to the prompt, replace the WordPerfect 1

disk in drive A with the WordPerfect 2 disk. The size of the letter or report you can write is limited to what will fit on the floppy disk in drive A.

If WordPerfect is loading correctly, you will see the WordPerfect opening screen, letting you know that everything is fine (see fig. 2.1).

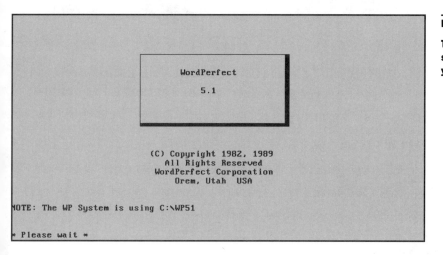

Fig. 2.1

The WordPerfect opening screen. If you see this, you did everything right!

Quitting WordPerfect

In Chapter 3, you learn how to save your letter or report to disk so that you can use it again at another time. Later in this chapter you will learn about WordPerfect's menus. In the meantime, when you need to quit the WordPerfect program, do the following:

1. Press Exit (the F7 function key).

2. In the lower left corner of the screen you'll see the message Save document? **Y**es (**N**o). Press N (for No).

3. A new message will appear: Exit WordPerfect? **N**o (**Y**es). Press Y (for Yes).

You have exited from (or quit) WordPerfect.

What if you have too little memory?

If you see the WordPerfect opening screen when you type *WP*, you can skip this section, because WordPerfect has found enough memory to operate successfully. However, when you start WordPerfect, you have a problem if you get the message: `Program too big to fit in memory`.

Your computer came with a certain amount of RAM–usually 640K or more. WordPerfect needs about 400K of that memory to run. (The program works better if you have at least 512K.) Having enough memory shouldn't be a problem unless you use an older computer, some of which are equipped with very little memory. If your computer is newer, it almost certainly has enough memory to run WordPerfect.

When you get the memory-error message, either you have too little memory in your computer and need to buy more, or you have other programs hogging memory that WordPerfect wants to use. There are many possible reasons for the memory-error message. Most of the solutions require some computer expertise. If you aren't sure what the problem is or how to fix it, call WordPerfect technical support at (800) 533-9605.

WordPerfect needs about 400K of memory. Most computers have at least that much.

Understanding WordPerfect's clean screen

The WordPerfect editing screen is clean, giving you lots of room to work.

Once WordPerfect is up and running, there isn't much to look at on your computer screen. You see only a small blinking line in the upper left and a status line at the bottom of the screen. The reason is that WordPerfect uses a "clean screen," also called WordPerfect's main editing screen. This screen leaves ample room for you to enter text.

The blinking underline in the upper left corner of the screen is the *cursor*. When you start typing, text appears on the screen right above and just to the left of the cursor. The cursor is where action takes place. As you type, the cursor moves from left to right across the screen. In Chapter 3, you will learn how to move the cursor around the screen.

At the bottom of the clean screen is the *status line*, shown in figure 2.2. The status line provides the following information:

✴ **The document's name**, if there is one; and where it's located. The name appears on the left side of the status line. For example, the name MYLETTER tells you that the letter you are writing or editing is called "Myletter."

✴ **WordPerfect messages**, such as * Please wait *. A WordPerfect message appears in the lower left corner of the status line.

✴ **The active document.** WordPerfect allows you to have two documents open at the same time. The right side of the status line tells you whether you have document 1 or 2 (Doc 1 or Doc 2) active.

✳ **The page number you are on.** This information appears on the right side of the status line.

✳ **The position of the cursor on the page.** The position is measured from the top (Ln) and left margin (Pos) of the page. This information is displayed on the right side of the status line.

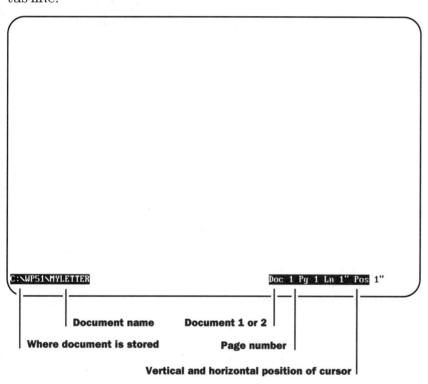

Fig. 2.2

The clean screen and the status line.

C:\WP51\MYLETTER   Doc 1 Pg 1 Ln 1" Pos 1"

Document name   Document 1 or 2

Where document is stored   Page number

Vertical and horizontal position of cursor

Understanding computer keyboards

The special keys on a computer keyboard pack a lot of power and convenience.

The keyboard on a computer is in some ways similar to a regular typewriter keyboard. Similarities include the way the space bar, Shift, Tab, Enter (or Return), alphabet, and number keys work. There are major differences, however, between the computer and typewriter keyboards (see fig. 2.3):

✳ **Special keys** appear on a computer keyboard that don't appear on most typewriter keyboards. Some special keys used by WordPerfect are Esc, Home, and the arrow keys.

✳ **Function keys** are labeled F1 through F10 or F12. The function keys can be pressed either individually or in conjunction with the Alt, Ctrl, or Shift key. For example, if you press and hold down the Ctrl key and then press F2, the combination is called Ctrl-F2.

✳ **Sequential keys** are pressed one after the other. For example, pressing and releasing the Home key and then pressing the left arrow is different from just pressing either Home or the left arrow.

Fig. 2.3

A typical PC keyboard and its special keys.

Esc key

Function (F1-F10 or F12) keys

Ctrl, Alt, and Shift keys

Cursor keys

Numeric keypad

Understanding menus

When you go into a restaurant, you are handed a menu. After you look over the choices, you make your selection, and (at the better restaurants) what you ordered soon appears in front of you on the table. Similarly, a *menu* in WordPerfect is a list of choices, presented on the computer screen, from which you make a selection. A simple menu might ask whether you want to quit the program. A complex menu might ask you to select from a number of options.

Just like in a restaurant, WordPerfect lists your choices by telling you what's on the menu.

Using a menu involves two steps. First you display or access the menu. Then you choose an item from the menu.

You *display or access a menu* in one of two ways: through pull-down menus or through function keys. Most new users find the pull-down menus easier to learn, but if you are a touch typist, you may find the function-key method a bit faster. Both methods will be explained shortly. You can use either one.

You *choose a menu item* in one of two ways, as well. You can press the highlighted letter or number that corresponds to your choice, or you can use a mouse. Using a mouse with the menus will be discussed shortly.

The next few pages explain more about menus. Unfortunately, there is not a simple way to jump into this topic, but I've broken the subject into "bite-sized" chunks for easier digestion. Once you've practiced the exercises in this chapter, you might want to reread this section to help reinforce what you have learned.

Understanding basic menu types

It would be nice if all WordPerfect's menus were identical,

but they're not. There are three basic types of menus in WordPerfect:

✲ **Status-line menus** appear on a single line at the bottom of your screen (see fig. 2.4). You can still see your WordPerfect document when the line menu appears. After you make a selection, the line menu disappears, and you are returned to the main editing screen.

Fig. 2.4

A line menu.

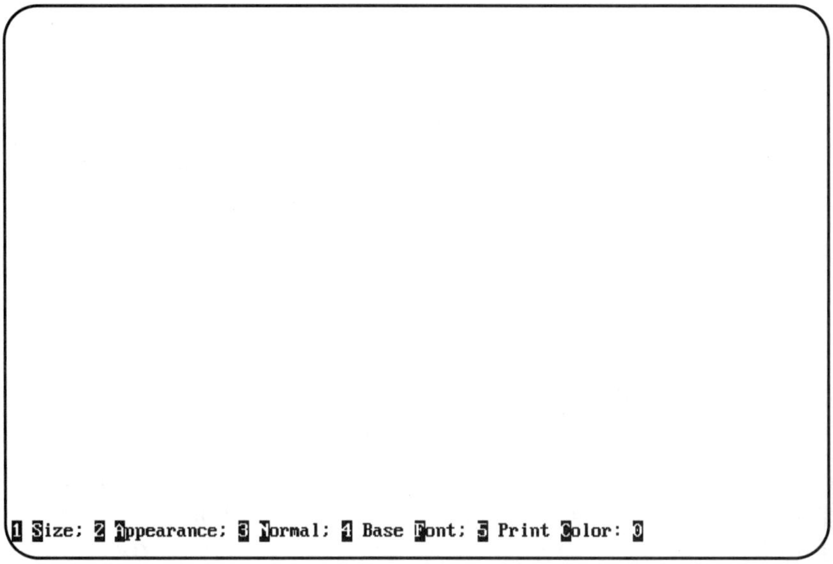
1 Size; 2 Appearance; 3 Normal; 4 Base Font; 5 Print Color: 0

✲ **Full-screen menus** cover the entire WordPerfect editing screen (see fig. 2.5). Usually, such a menu remains on the screen, allowing you to make more than one choice. To return to the main editing screen, you usually need to press Exit (F7) or the right mouse button.

✲ **Nested menus** (whether line or full-screen) lead to other menus. The final choices you make are from the "nested" menus. With some nested menus, making the selection takes you to the main editing screen. With others, you must press Exit (F7) one or more times to return to the main editing screen. Pressing Cancel (F1) or Esc either returns you to the main editing screen or takes you up one level in the nest without making any changes.

```
┌────────────────────────────────────────────────────────────┐
│ Format                                                       │
│                                                              │
│    1 - Line                                                  │
│            Hyphenation              Line Spacing             │
│            Justification            Margins Left/Right       │
│            Line Height              Tab Set                  │
│            Line Numbering           Widow/Orphan Protection  │
│                                                              │
│    2 - Page                                                  │
│            Center Page (top to bottom)  Page Numbering       │
│            Force Odd/Even Page          Paper Size/Type/Labels│
│            Headers and Footers          Suppress            │
│            Margins Top/Bottom                               │
│                                                              │
│    3 - Document                                             │
│            Display Pitch            Redline Method          │
│            Initial Codes/Font       Summary                 │
│                                                              │
│    4 - Other                                                │
│            Advance                  Printer Functions       │
│            Conditional End of Page  Underline Spaces/Tabs   │
│            Decimal Characters       Border Options          │
│            Language                 End Centering/Alignment │
│            Overstrike                                       │
│ Selection: 0                                                │
└────────────────────────────────────────────────────────────┘
```

Fig. 2.5

A full-screen menu.

Regardless of the type of menu, you make choices from a
list. Each item on the list usually has a letter and number highlighted. (The letter choices usually correspond to the first letter of the menu option. This arrangement helps make the
command easier to remember. Such letter commands are
called *mnemonics*.)

To make a selection, press the highlighted letter or number
that corresponds to your choice. Or, if you have a mouse, you
can move the mouse cursor over the choice and click the left
mouse button to make the selection. In any of these menus, if
you are using a mouse, pressing the right mouse button has the
same effect as pressing Exit (F7). Pressing both the left and
right (or middle, on a three-button mouse) buttons at the
same time has the same effect as pressing Cancel (F1).

Using the pull-down menu bar

The pull-down menu bar appears across the top of the
WordPerfect screen when you press the Alt-= combination
(see fig. 2.6). If you have a mouse, pressing the right mouse
button activates the pull-down menu bar with its nine choices.
The way the pull-down menu is displayed gives it its name.
Just like a window shade that rolls open when you pull on the
cord, these pull-down menus "roll" down the screen, making

all their choices visible at once.

When you press Alt-=, the **F**ile pull-down menu item is highlighted. You can reveal the pull-down menu in one of several ways:

✲ Press the highlighted letter of the menu item (for example, L for **L**ayout or F for **F**ile).

✲ Press the right or left arrow until the menu item you want is highlighted then either press the down arrow or press Enter.

✲ If you have a mouse, position the mouse cursor over the menu item and press the left mouse button.

✲ If a pull-down menu item offers additional choices, a right-facing triangle appears next to the item. When that menu item is highlighted, a secondary menu "pops out." You navigate the pop-out menu the same way you do the pull-down menu.

✲ If a pull-down menu has choices that aren't available, they will appear in brackets.

Fig. 2.6

The pull-down menu bar.

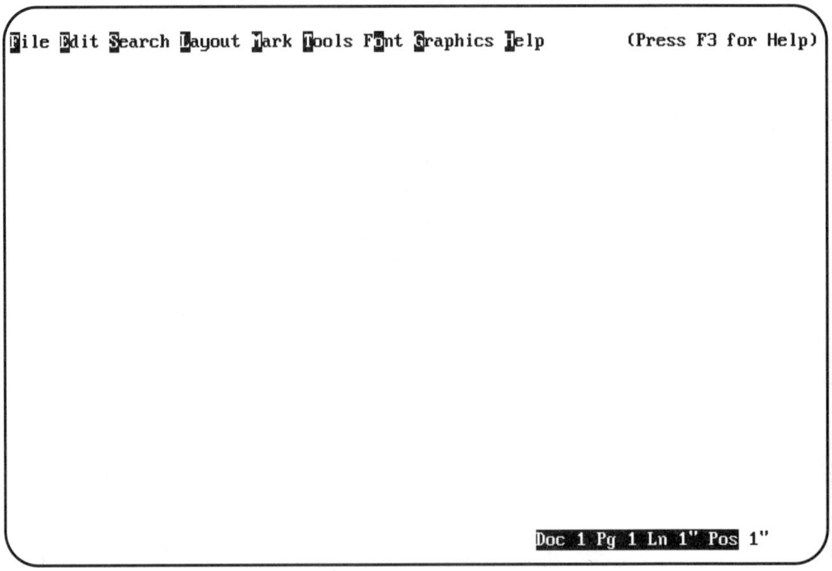

To access, for example, the Justify menu, do the following:

1. Press Alt-= to activate the menu bar.

2. Press L for **L**ayout to activate the pull-down menu (see fig. 2.7).

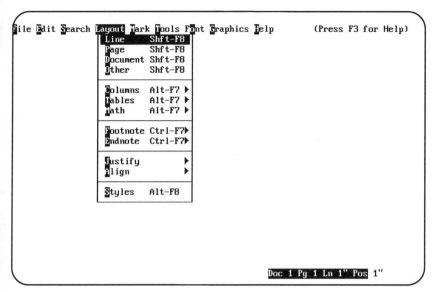

Fig. 2.7

The Layout pull-down menu.

3. Press J for **J**ustify to activate the pop-out menu (see fig. 2.8).

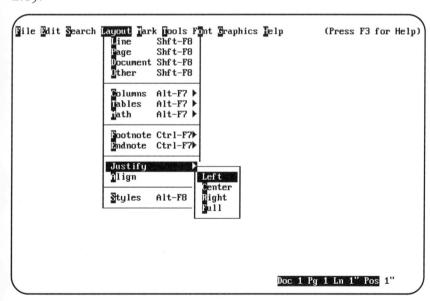

Fig. 2.8

The Justify pop-out menu.

4. To "back out" of the menus one step at a time (without making any changes), press the Esc key three times.

Making a selection from a pull-down menu

Once you have activated a pull-down menu, you can make

your choice in one of several ways:

✳ Using the up and down arrows, move the cursor up or down the menu until your choice is highlighted and then press Enter.

✳ Press the highlighted letter of the menu item (for example, P for **P**rint).

✳ If you have a mouse, highlight the menu item of your choice with the mouse cursor then press the left mouse button.

Leaving the pull-down menu bar permanently visible

If you prefer having the pull-down menus visible all the time, do the following steps:

1. Press Setup (Shift-F1) and then select **2** - **D**isplay

or

Choose **F**ile, then Se**t**up, and then **D**isplay from menu.

2. Select **4** - **M**enu Options.

3. From the Setup: Menu Options screen, choose **8** - Menu Bar Remains **V**isible.

4. From the **N**o (**Y**es) prompt, press Y (for Yes) or choose **Y**es with the mouse.

5. Press Exit (F7) to return to the editing screen.

The pull-down menu bar will remain visible. If you change your mind and don't want the menu bar visible all the time, perform the steps just given, but press N (for No) in Step 4. Even if the menu bar isn't visible, you can still access it at any time by pressing Alt-=.

One thing to remember: You can do the same things in WordPerfect through either the function-key combinations or the pull-down menus. You can do the same things with or without a mouse. With a few exceptions, the function keys and pull-down menus act as gateways to the ultimate menus or prompts from which you will make choices. The ultimate menus or prompts are the same regardless of whether you get to them by using the function keys or the pull-down menus.

Adding a separator line to the pull-down menu bar

On many displays, the menu bar is not very distinctive and blends in with the text. You can distinguish the menu bar by adding a separator line (see fig. 2.9).

File Edit Search Layout Mark Tools Font Graphics Help   (Press F3 for Help)

Doc 1 Pg 1 Ln 1" Pos 1"

Fig. 2.9

The pull-down menu bar with a separator line.

To add the separator line, make the following keystrokes and selections: Setup (Shift-F1), **2** - **D**isplay, **4** - **M**enu Options, **7** - Menu Bar **S**eparator Line, **Y**es, Exit (F7).

Accessing the menus with the function keys

If you are a touch typist, you may prefer the function-key method of accessing menus. Although the pull-down menus are easier to learn, if you will be using WordPerfect a lot, you may well opt for the function-key approach because it is usually faster once you've mastered it.

There are 10 function keys (12 if you have an enhanced keyboard), and each key can be pressed alone or with the Shift, Ctrl, or Alt key (see the next section about printing the function-key template). WordPerfect uses 40 function-key combinations. The program makes such complete use of the function keys that they are often called by WordPerfect's name for them. For example, F1 is also the Cancel key.

If you use the function keys, you will eventually memorize

what most of them do. In the meantime, you will find it helpful to tape to your keyboard the plastic function-key template that came with your copy of WordPerfect.

Printing a function-key template

If you have lost the template, you can print one out directly from WordPerfect. To print a template, do the following steps:

1. Press Help (F3) twice.

2. If your keyboard's function keys are on the left, press 1. If your keyboard's function keys are across the top, skip to Step 3.

3. Press the Print Screen key. The template on the screen will be printed by your printer (see fig. 2.10).

4. Cut out the template and place it next to your keyboard for easy reference.

Fig. 2.10

The WordPerfect template for the enhanced keyboard.

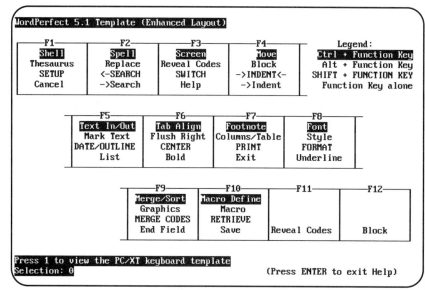

```
WordPerfect 5.1 Template (Enhanced Layout)

   ―F1―          ―F2―          ―F3―          ―F4―             Legend:
   Shell         Spell         Screen        Move        Ctrl + Function Key
   Thesaurus     Replace       Reveal Codes  Block        Alt + Function Key
   SETUP         <-SEARCH       SWITCH       ->INDENT<-   SHIFT + FUNCTION KEY
   Cancel        ->Search       Help         ->Indent       Function Key alone

                ―F5―          ―F6―          ―F7―          ―F8―
                Text In/Out   Tab Align     Footnote      Font
                Mark Text     Flush Right   Columns/Table Style
                DATE/OUTLINE  CENTER        PRINT         FORMAT
                List          Bold          Exit          Underline

                             ―F9―          ―F10―         ―F11―         ―F12―
                             Merge/Sort     Macro Define
                             Graphics       Macro
                             MERGE CODES    RETRIEVE
                             End Field      Save         Reveal Codes   Block

Press 1 to view the PC/XT keyboard template
Selection: 0                                      (Press ENTER to exit Help)
```

If you use the original templates, you will notice that they are color-coded (red = Ctrl, blue = Alt, green = Shift, and black = unmodified). If you place color dots on the Ctrl, Alt, and Shift keys, they will help remind you which modifier key to press along with the function key to access the appropriate menu. (If you use a template you print yourself, use a colored pen to color-code it.)

Examining a typical menu

You can use this book whether you choose to access the menus through the pull-down menus or the function keys. Each time examples are given that require menu choices, you're told how to use either approach to get to the right menu. Function keys are designated by both the function-key number and the WordPerfect name for the function key.

Here's an example of how a typical menu–the Spell menu– works. WordPerfect has the capability to double-check your document for correct spelling. To check your document for any misspelled words, do the following:

1. Press Spell (Ctrl-F2)

or

Choose Sp**e**ll from the **T**ools menu.

2. Choose from the following choices displayed at the bottom of the screen:

```
Check: 1 Word 2 Page 3 Document 4 New Sup.
Dictionary 5 Look Up 6 Count: 0
```

These six choices form the menu for Spell. As already explained, most menus in WordPerfect give you the option of pressing either a number or a letter to make a menu selection. For example, you could press either 1 or W to spell-check a single word. Letter choices are usually the first letter of the word (although not always) and are highlighted on your computer screen.

In most menus, if you change your mind and don't want to make any choice, you can press 0 most of the time. If that doesn't work, you can try Cancel (F1), Esc, or Exit (F7). If you have a mouse, pressing the right button is the same as pressing Exit (F7) pressing the left and right buttons at the same time (or the middle button if you have a three-button mouse) is the same as pressing Cancel (F1).

Accessing the menu and then making your choice are the two steps to telling WordPerfect what you want it to do.

Changing your mind in menus

If you make a mistake or change your mind, it's okay.

WordPerfect is very forgiving and will let you make a correction. Depending on the menu, there are several ways to make a change:

✻ Press Cancel (F1) to deactivate the menu. If you are in a nested menu, you press Cancel (F1) for each menu level until you are back at the main editing screen.

✻ If you have a mouse, hold down the left mouse button and then click the right mouse button. This is the same as pressing Cancel (F1). If your mouse has three buttons, pressing the middle button is the same as pressing Cancel (F1).

✻ Some menus remain on the screen, allowing you to make several choices. In these menus, if you make a mistake, you can reselect the menu item and make the correction.

✻ In some menus, once you choose an item, the change is made and you are immediately returned to the editing screen. The easiest way to correct mistakes in these menus is to retrace your steps and make the correct choice.

✻ If the menu choice you have made has inserted a hidden code (see the section later in this chapter), you can undo your action by deleting the hidden code.

✻ If you are using the pull-down menus, you can back up one step by pressing the Esc key.

Getting help

Many believe that WordPerfect has the best on-line Help of any software program. Help is never very far away in WordPerfect. Every single feature you can use has an explanation that can appear instantly on-screen. One way to have fun learning about WordPerfect is to play with the Help function.

With WordPerfect, Help is only a keystroke away. Whenever you're lost or lonely, press Help (F3).

To use Help, keep the following in mind:

✳ If you are in a menu, pressing Help (F3) brings up a context-sensitive Help screen. That means that the information you see will relate to the menu you are using. WordPerfect provides help appropriate to whatever you're trying to accomplish at the moment. For example, if you have chosen the Format: Page menu and are confused about the menu options, pressing Help (F3) provides assistance relevant to the Format: Page menu choices.

✳ If you are in the main editing screen, pressing Help (F3) or choosing **H**elp from the **H**elp pull-down menu launches the Help feature. From here, either you can press a function key to find out more about what its features are, or you can press a letter of the alphabet to see an alphabetical listing of all of WordPerfect's features that begin with that letter.

✳ Once the Help function is active, you can press any function key to learn more about that particular key, or you can press a letter key for an index of features. You can move from Help screen to Help screen as long as you want. When you want to return to the main editing screen, press Enter.

✳ Try pressing the following keys, which have their own Help screens: arrow keys, Ctrl-arrow keys, Home, PgUp, PgDn, End, Tab, Shift-Tab, Esc, Hyphen, Insert, Delete, Ctrl-V, Backspace, GoTo (Ctrl-Home), Ctrl-PgUp, Ctrl-PgDn, and Ctrl-End.

✳ Pressing Help (F3) twice or choosing **T**emplate from the **H**elp menu summons an on-screen representation of the enhanced keyboard function-key assignments. You press 1 from this screen to see the regular keyboard function-key assignments.

For example, to learn more about justification, do the following:

1. Press Help (F3)

or

Choose **H**elp or **I**ndex from the **H**elp menu.

2. Press J (the first letter of *Justification*).

Typing a letter of the alphabet (like J) brings up an alphabetical list of all the WordPerfect features (see fig. 2.11).

Fig. 2.11

An index of WordPerfect features that begin with the letters J and K.

Features [J-K]	WordPerfect Key	Keystrokes
Justification	Format	Shft-F8,1,3
Justification Limits	Format	Shft-F8,4,6,4
Keep Lines Together	Format	Shft-F8,4,2
Kerning	Format	Shft-F8,4,6,1
Keyboard Definitions/Layout	Setup	Shft-F1,5
Keyboard/Macro Files	Setup	Shft-F1,6,2
Keyboard Map	Setup	Shft-F1,5,8

Selection: 0   (Press ENTER to exit Help)

3. To learn more about justification, press the keystroke combination listed in the right-hand column. In this case, press Shift-F8, 1, and 3.

4. You should see the justification Help screen shown in figure 2.12. To return to a menu or the main editing screen from Help, press Enter or the space bar.

Fig. 2.12

The justification
Help screen.

```
┌─────────────────────────────────────────────────────────────────────╮
│ Justification                                                          │
│                                                                        │
│   Allows you to specify how text should be aligned with respect to the left │
│   and right margins.  WordPerfect inserts a code at the cursor location.    │
│   If your cursor is not at the left margin when you set justification,      │
│   [DSRt] is inserted before the setting. Text in the document is justified  │
│   as you have indicated until you insert another code that changes the      │
│   setting.                                                                  │
│                                                                            │
│   Left - Aligns text against left margin, leaving right margin ragged.      │
│                                                                            │
│   Center - Centers text between margins.  The result is similar to centering│
│        each line of text using Center (Shift-F6).  When you block lines of  │
│        text and press Center, WordPerfect inserts a [Just: Center] code     │
│        before the text and a [Just:] code after the text that returns the   │
│        justification to its original setting.  Should you alter             │
│        justification above the centered text, you may have to manually      │
│        change the [Just:] code after the centered text.                     │
│                                                                            │
│   Right - Aligns text against right margin, leaves left margin ragged.      │
│                                                                            │
│   Full - Aligns text against right and left margins.  The result is the     │
│        same as the Right Justification familiar to WordPerfect 5.0 users.   │
│                                                                            │
│ Selection: 0                                  (Press ENTER to exit Help)    │
└─────────────────────────────────────────────────────────────────────╯
```

Notes

_____

_____

_____

_____

_____

_____

_____

_____

2|36 Learning about hidden codes

Hidden codes are inserted into your document when you change settings (like margins and tabs) or format text (like bold or underline).

While confusing, you must learn about hidden codes to use WordPerfect effectively.

Most users of WordPerfect agree that the concept of hidden codes is one of the most difficult to grasp and work with. However, to use WordPerfect you need to understand hidden codes.

When you use a typewriter to create a letter, you set margins and tabs and otherwise specify how you want the page to look once you're done. This is called *formatting*. With a word processor such as WordPerfect, formatting is done electronically. The following are examples of formatting:

* Margin and tab settings
* Paper size
* Text attributes like <u>underlining</u> and **boldfacing**
* Font size like large and small
* Tabs and indents

Whenever you give WordPerfect formatting instructions, a formatting instruction code is inserted into your document. To keep the clean screen from becoming cluttered and confusing, WordPerfect hides the codes unless you want to look at them.

Perform the following steps to learn more about hidden codes:

1. Type the following:

This sentence will help demonstrate how hidden codes work and what they look like on-screen.

Press Enter.

2. Press Reveal Codes (Alt-F3)

or

Choose **R**eveal Codes from the **E**dit menu.

A window appears below the main editing screen. In that window you can see the same text as is in the main editing screen. The difference is that in the reveal codes window, you see not just the text but also hidden formatting codes.

For example, at the end of the first line (where the text automatically wraps around to the next line) is a bracketed and boldfaced symbol–the code **[SRt]**. (This code means "soft return" and is inserted at the end of each line to tell WordPerfect to move the next word to the next line.) As another example, when you pressed the hyphen key to punctuate the word *on-screen*, WordPerfect inserted the hyphen code, **[-]**.

3. At the end of the sentence, where you pressed Enter, WordPerfect inserted the **[HRt]** code. (This code means "hard return" and is inserted whenever you press Enter.) To watch WordPerfect insert another **[HRt]** code, press Enter.

4. Press Tab. When you do so, WordPerfect inserts the hidden code **[Tab]**, which is visible in the reveal codes window. In the main editing window, the cursor moves to the right.

5. Press Bold (F6) and type *This is bold text*. Press Bold (F6) a second time. Notice that the text in the upper screen appears in bold. In the reveal codes window, the text itself isn't bold, but pressing the Bold (F6) key inserted two hidden codes–**[Bold]** and **[bold]**–and the text you typed in the reveal codes window is bracketed by those codes.

Look at figure 2.13 to see the hidden codes you've entered so far.

Understanding the effect of hidden codes

Codes are inserted either with single keystrokes (as with Tab or hyphen) or as the result of a choice you make on a menu. The following are several categories of hidden codes:

✳ **Codes that affect the rest of a document.** Some hidden codes affect only the text that comes after them. For example, if you insert a top-margin change on page 2 of your letter, only page 2 and following pages have a new top margin. Page 1 is not affected.

```
┌─────────────────────────────────────────────────────────────┐
│ This sentence will help demonstrate how hidden codes work and │
│ what they look like on-screen                                 │
│                                                               │
│     This is bold text                                         │
│                                                               │
│                                                               │
│                                                               │
│                                              Doc 1 Pg 1 Ln 1.5" Pos 3.2" │
│ {    ▲    ▲    ▲    ▲    ▲    ▲    ▲    ▲    ▲    ▲    } ▲    ▲  │
│ This sentence will help demonstrate how hidden codes work and[SRt] │
│ what they look like on[-]screen[HRt]                          │
│ [HRt]                                                         │
│ [Tab][BOLD]This is bold text[bold]                            │
│                                                               │
│                                                               │
│ Press Reveal Codes to restore screen                          │
└─────────────────────────────────────────────────────────────┘
```

Fig. 2.13.

Hidden codes.

❊ **Codes that give a single instruction.** Some codes give a single instruction to do a single thing (like "advance 3 inches down" or "insert today's date" or "tab") and don't have any further effect.

❊ **Codes that act like "on" and "off" switches.** Some hidden codes act like "on" and "off" switches. For example, when you want something in bold, you press the Bold (F6) key to insert a "bold-on code" that turns bold on. When you are finished with bold, you press the Bold (F6) key again to move past a "bold-off code" that turns bold off.

❊ **Codes that are placeholders.** Some hidden codes are really pointers or placeholders for other information. For example, if you insert a header into your document, a **[Header]** code is inserted. This code contains all the information about the header, including the actual text of the header.

❊ **Codes that correspond to keystrokes.** Some hidden codes indicate a special keystroke. For example, pressing the hyphen inserts **[-]**, pressing Tab inserts **[Tab],** and pressing Enter inserts **[HRt].**

❊ **Codes that mark a location.** Some hidden codes mark a location for advanced WordPerfect operations like indexing and creating a table of contents.

Editing hidden codes

Hidden codes can be deleted, just like any text character. If the codes are hidden, you will usually be asked to confirm that you really want to delete the code before it is deleted.

Practice deleting some codes by doing the following:

1. Using the text you typed just now, press Backspace to delete the **[bold]** code. Notice that both the **[BOLD]** and **[bold]** codes are deleted and that the text in the main editing screen is no longer bold.

2. Press Backspace a number of times to delete the text up to the **[Tab]** code. Now press Backspace once more to delete the **[Tab]** code. Notice that the cursor jumps back to the left margin.

3. If you are not in reveal codes and you try deleting some codes, you'll be asked to confirm the deletion. For example, press Bold (F6). Now hide the reveal codes window by pressing Reveal Codes (Shift-F3). Now press Backspace. You will see the following prompt: `Delete [BOLD]? No (Yes)`. Press Y (for Yes).

When the codes are revealed, you are not asked to confirm any deletion (as in Step 1 when you deleted the **[bold]** code). Some codes (like **[Tab]**) don't require confirmation when you delete them, regardless of whether the codes are hidden or revealed.

Even though the code has more than one letter in it, Word-Perfect treats it like a single character for the purpose of deleting it. In the case of the **[Tab]** hidden code, a single keystroke can delete it. In the case of codes that have both an "on" and an "off" part, like **[BOLD]** and **[bold]**, deleting one of the pair deletes both.

You should know about hidden codes for several reasons:

✻ If you accidentally insert a code (like **[BOLD]**) and you don't want text boldfaced, you need to find and delete the unwanted code.

✻ If you want to change a code (for example, to modify the margin settings), you need to delete the old code and put a new code in its place.

✱ Some codes, especially those concerning placeholder codes like a header, can be edited. This process is explained in Chapter 7.

Notes

_____

_____

_____

_____

_____

_____

_____

_____

_____

_____

_____

_____

_____

_____

_____

Understanding defaults

Every time you start WordPerfect, the program automatically checks more than 100 settings–from margin settings and paper size to whether you want the pull-down menus displayed or whether you want documents automatically backed up. Most of the default settings that will be of interest to you are those that control formatting–how the document looks (margins, tab settings, font selection, spacing, justification, and so forth).

Life is too short to spend it telling WordPerfect your wishes concerning these settings every time you sit down to create a document. To save you time and trouble, WordPerfect comes with each of these 100-plus items preset to their most common settings. These presets are called *defaults*. Figure 2.14 shows a diagram of some of WordPerfect's defaults.

Defaults specify the way you want something done all the time. WordPerfect allows you to *override* the defaults any time you like. If you decide you like the override better than the default, you can change the default to reflect your new choice. In coming chapters you will learn how to do that. If you are interested in a more detailed discussion of defaults, see Appendix A.

Defaults are WordPerfect's way of saving you time. The basics are preset.

Willamette Rentals

June 27, 1991

Ms. Gail Wilson
2122 SE 32nd
Willamette, OR 97055

fully justified text

Dear Ms. Wilson,

As you know, once a year we evaluate the rental market in Willamette and take a look at our expenses. Almost always this requires us to have a slight rent increase. This year, the increases average less than 6% which is under the increase in inflation and well below the increase in the cost of property in the Willamette metro area (one of the hottest real estate markets in the United States).

In anticipation of the reductions in property taxes the state will see over the next five years, and because of the increased values of property in our area, the county significantly increased the assessed property values (averaging between 20-30%) this past year. This meant we paid hundreds of dollars more in taxes last year on the house you live in than we paid the year before.

1 inch left margin

In addition, our expenses in maintaining the houses and the general rise in the cost of doing business also played a role in our decision to reluctantly increase your monthly rent.

1 inch right margin

Fortunately, the voters of Oregon passed Proposition 5 this year, which will gradually reduce property taxes over a 5 year period. Unfortunately, the increased assessment has already taken place and is in effect for the current and subsequent tax years. This strategy of the county's greatly undercuts the savings that Proposition 5 would have generated.

Even so, as the benefits of Proposition 5 come into play, we will be able to take that into account each year when we re-evaluate the rents in the Willamette area. We hope that the slowing of rising property taxes will allow us to hold the rents more steady in the next year.

For your home, starting in August 1, 1991, the discounted monthly rent will increase $35.00 from $485.00 to $520.00. This is a 6% increase. Your house will not be subject to a rent review for at least another 12 months. Thank you for your cooperation and understanding. We appreciate your renting from us.

Yours truly,
Willamette Rentals

single spaced

Fig. 2.14

A diagram of a letter showing common WordPerfect default settings.

paper size 8.5 by 11 inches, tabs .5 inch

1 inch bottom margin

Chapter 3: Basic text editing

In the last chapter, you learned about installing WordPerfect and how to start and quit. You also learned about WordPerfect's unique clean screen. You were acquainted with the different menu types you'll encounter in the program and how to make selections using either the function keys or a mouse and the pull-down menu. You then learned about hidden formatting codes, what they affect, and how to edit them.

In this chapter, you'll type your first letter using WordPerfect. You'll save and retrieve the document. You'll learn how to move around the page using the cursor keys or the mouse (you'll also learn some great shortcuts).

Finally, you'll learn some basic editing

By the time you finish this chapter, you'll know how to "navigate" and do basic editing in a WordPerfect document.

techniques, including deleting and undeleting text; and how to substitute one word for another using the thesaurus.

Be sure to do the examples as they're explained, and by the time you finish this section, you will be able to create a letter in WordPerfect.

Notes

_____

_____

_____

_____

_____

_____

_____

_____

_____

_____

_____

Entering text

Typing a letter in WordPerfect is not much different from typing a letter on a typewriter. First start WordPerfect, then begin by typing the sample text shown in figure 3.1. Don't worry about errors or how to correct them–you'll learn how to fix those later in the chapter.

Now, down to some work.

Type the sample letter as shown. You'll use it in this and other chapters.

A few things to remember:

✳ Don't press Enter (the equivalent of the Return key on a typewriter) except at the end of a paragraph. WordPerfect automatically fits as many words on a line as it can. If a word won't fit, WordPerfect automatically "wraps" (or moves) the word to the beginning of the next line.

✳ Don't worry about misspellings or typographical errors. You'll learn how to correct those later.

✳ Press the space bar only once (not twice) after periods.

✳ Don't worry if some of the lines end in different places on your screen than they do in the figure. Your printer may be different from mine, and the calculations WordPerfect makes for how long a line can be are based (in large part) on what kind of printer you use.

✳ Make the letter as much like the example as you can. Intentional mistakes are included so that you will have something to fix later

Congratulations! You've just typed your first letter in Word-Perfect.

Press Enter twice before the salutation (to leave room for the date later)

Don't press Enter at the ends of lines. Let WordPerfect "wrap" the line.

Dear Mitch,

It was great you and Jeff could come up for the weekend. We enjoyed your company. The only problem is the visit was too short.

Misspell these words.

Type this word twice.

We reelly liked Jeff's ideas about the liiving room room. After his explanation, it became clear that the fireplace should be the focal point of the living room. In order to do that, we now need to look for two new sofas instead of one!

Our old house finally sold, so we will soon have the money to work with for purchasing new living room furniture.

Press Enter twice to double-space between paragraphs.

Would you please ask him if he thinks we should try and get the furniture to match the carpet or consider an Oriental rug and then try and match the furniture to it? To refresh his memory, we had looked at pattern H7122.

We'll hold you to your promise to visit again before the end of summer.

Yours truly,

Skye and Jane

Fig. 3.1.
The sample LETTER.1.

Entering the date automatically

In the sample letter, you could have entered the date manually–that is, by typing it in. But why do that when Word-Perfect will automatically enter it for you? The "automatic date" feature is one of the most fun things WordPerfect knows how to do, and the feature saves you time as well.

All letters need dates.

Let WordPerfect do the work for you.

You can practice entering the date automatically by placing the cursor at the top of the document (press Home, Home, and Enter) and doing the following:

Press Date/Outline (Shift-F5) and choose **1** Date **T**ext

or

Choose Date **T**ext from the **T**ools menu.

WordPerfect will automatically enter the date as "month date, year"–for example, "June 16, 1991." (Although it may never be necessary, you can change the way WordPerfect enters the date by changing the date format. Consult your Word-Perfect manual to learn how to do this.)

If you want WordPerfect to update the date every time you retrieve the document, then instead of choosing **1** Date **T**ext, choose **2** Date **C**ode to insert a date code (**[Date:3 1, 4]**). The document will then have a "live" date that is updated to the *current* date every time you open or print the document.

Using
Save (F10)

Because later you're going to use the letter you just typed, you need to save it. To save the letter, do the following:

1. Press Save (F10)

or

Choose **S**ave from the **F**ile menu.

2. At the `Document to be saved:` prompt, type *LETTER. 1* to give the file a name, and then press Enter. (See the next section for information on how to name files.)

The status line will ask you to wait (`* Please wait *`) while WordPerfect is saving the file. Once the file has been saved, the status line will tell you the name of the file and where on your computer it's stored.

After the file is saved, the status line should say

`C:\WP51\LETTER.1`

The status line is telling you the name of the document (LETTER.1) and where it can be found (C:\WP51). The name of the document is called the *file name*, the location where it can be found is called a *directory* or *path*. (Note: The path on your computer may be different from C:\WP51\.)

You can change the directory where WordPerfect stores your document files, but how to do this is an advanced topic beyond the scope of this book. If you find that you need to change the directory, read about changing the location of files in the WordPerfect manual.

Understanding file naming

In Step 2 in the preceding section, you named the document *LETTER. 1*. The operating system for IBM-compatible computers lets you give files almost any name you choose, provided that you follow some simple rules:

File names can only be 8 letters (plus a 3-letter extension) long.

✽ The file name can have up to eight letters, then a period, and then up to three more letters. (The final three letters are called an *extension*.) You don't need to use all eight letters, and you don't need to have an extension.

✽ The file name can use any letter or number and most (but not all) of the punctuation characters, such as ! @ # $ % ^ & ( ) _ + - { } ~ ' '.

✽ The file name can't have any spaces, question marks, commas, tabs, or asterisks.

✽ The file name can't use special characters that have a meaning to the operating system, such as / : \ | < > + [ ] ".

✽ The operating system automatically converts all lowercase letters to capital letters, so you can't have lowercase letters in a file name.

A tip on naming files: Because you are limited to eight letters plus a three-letter extension, you will want to develop a logical file-naming procedure. For example, if you regularly send out bids, you might want to make the first part of the file name (up to eight letters) the customer name and make the extension BID. So a bid for the Wellstar Company would be filed under WELLSTAR.BID a bid for Hammersmith, Inc., would be filed under HAMMERSM.BID.

Another type of letter might be regular correspondence to

the same person or company. For example, you might send regular letters to Mary Jones. To keep track of which letter is which, you could use her name as the first part of the file name and use either a date or a sequence for the extension. So MJONES.591 could be a letter to Mary Jones written in May of 1991, MJONES.510 could be a letter written May 10, and MJONES.3 could be the third letter you've written to her.

Whatever makes the most sense to you will make life easier when you need to hunt up a letter or report. Think about the way you file your documents, and jot down the rules so that you (and others using your system) will follow a standard naming procedure.

Notes

Saving a document using Exit (F7)

When you use the Save (F10) key, the document you are typing remains on-screen. If after saving the document you want to start again with a clean screen, do the following:

1. Press Exit (F7)

or

Choose E**x**it from the **F**ile menu.

2. At the `Save document: Yes (No):` prompt, press Y.

3. At the `Document to be saved:` prompt, enter the file name.

If there is already a file with that name, you will see the prompt: `Replace C:\WP51\<filename>? No (Yes)` (where <filename> is the file name you typed in).

If you press N, you'll be returned to the `Document to be saved:` prompt. You can then type a new file name for your document.

If you press Y, you will replace the file on the disk with the file you are currently editing.

4. At the `Exit WP? No (Yes)` prompt, press N.

The file has been saved, and you now have a clean screen.

You can do two other things at Step 4. If you press Cancel (F1), the document you just saved will remain on-screen. If you press Y, you will quit WordPerfect.

Here's another way to save files.

Which do you prefer?

Using Retrieve (Shift-F10)

If you know the name of the file, you can use Retrieve (Shift-F10).

Once a document has been saved, you can retrieve it from the disk in one of two ways: with Retrieve (Shift-F10) or with List Files (F5).

To retrieve a file by using Retrieve (Shift-F10), do the following:

1. Press Retrieve (Shift-F10)

or

Choose **R**etrieve from the **F**ile menu.

2. At the Document to be retrieved: prompt, type *LETTER.1*. If you don't know the file name, you could use F5 (List Files). The next section discusses this feature.

3. Press Enter.

The sample letter should now be back on-screen.

If the file doesn't exist or you typed the wrong path or file name, you'll see the error message ERROR: File not found. The Document to be retrieved: prompt reappears with the erroneous file name still in place. You can correct the error by either editing or replacing the document name and then pressing Enter again.

When you retrieved a document, if the main editing screen was empty, the name of the document you retrieved will appear on the status line. If you retrieved another document into a document you were already editing, the file name won't change (or if no name was previously given, there will still be no file name until you save the document).

Using List Files (F5)

WordPerfect has a built-in file manager that has a number of capabilities. One is the capability to help you when you can't remember either the name of a file or what exactly is in a file you want to retrieve.

If you don't know the name of the file, use WordPerfect's List Files (F5) function.

To use List Files to retrieve LETTER.1, do the following:

1. Press List Files (F5)

or

Choose List **F**iles from the **F**ile menu.

2. You will see a prompt that tells you what your current directory is. This directory may vary from system to system. For example, if all of your files were installed into the C:\WP51 directory, the prompt would read Dir C:\WP51*.*.

At this point, you can edit the path or type a new path name. (If you want to change the default path permanently, until you quit WordPerfect, then press the equal [=] key before typing a new path name.)

3. Press Enter. The List Files screen (see fig. 3.2) appears.

4. Using the cursor keys, move the cursor bar from file name to file name until LETTER.1 is highlighted.

Note: If there are several files, you can do a name search for the document by selecting **N N**ame Search and then typing a few letters of the file name. Once the cursor is on the correct file name, press Enter. Pressing the arrow keys deactivates Name Search.

5. At this point you can do several things. Two activities in particular are relevant at this point:

✳ By choosing either **6 L**ook or Enter, you can look at the contents of the document without first retrieving it. Looking at a document is useful if you can't remember or aren't sure what's in it. Inside the Look window, you can read through the text. If you want to see other parts of the document, you can use many of the keyboard shortcuts. You cannot do any editing in the Look window. When you're finished looking, press Exit (F7). (If you see a lot of nonsense, when you use Look to view a file, you probably are trying to look at a program file. If this happens, just press Exit [F7] to return to the List Files screen.)

✳ You can retrieve a document by choosing **1 R**etrieve. (If you already have some text in the main editing screen, Word-Perfect issues the prompt Retrieve into current document? **N**o (**Y**es). If you want to combine the document you are retrieving with the document you were working on, press Y. If you forgot you were working on something and don't want to combine documents, press N.

Fig. 3.2

The List Files screen, showing the file names, the size of the files (in kilobytes), and the date and time they were created or last edited.

```
07-10-91  02:10p              Directory C:\WP51\*.*
Document size:          0   Free: 73,531,392 Used:   3,687,230    Files:      68

  INSTALL .EXE    62,992  05-31-91 12:00p ▲ KEYS    .MRS    4,800  05-31-91 12:00p
  LETTER  .1       1,196  07-10-91 02:10p   MACROCNV.EXE   27,039  05-31-91 12:00p
  MYLETTER.          325  07-08-91 09:53a   NWPSETUP.EXE   28,672  05-31-91 12:00p
  PARADISE.VRS    15,256  05-31-91 12:00p   PRINTER .TST    8,665  05-31-91 12:00p
  README  .SEM         0  10-24-90 03:58p   README  .VRS   12,938  08-07-90 12:00p
  README  .WP     13,110  06-29-90 12:00p   SPELL   .EXE   56,320  05-31-91 12:00p
  STANDARD.CRS     2,555  05-31-91 12:00p   STANDARD.IRS    4,905  05-31-91 12:00p
  STANDARD.PRS     1,942  05-31-91 12:00p   STANDARD.VRS   30,482  05-31-91 12:00p
  TIGA    .DOC     1,505  08-07-90 12:00p   TIGA    .VRS   22,888  08-07-90 12:00p
  VGA512  .FRS     4,096  05-31-91 12:00p   VGAITAL .FRS    4,096  05-31-91 12:00p
  VGASMC  .FRS     4,096  05-31-91 12:00p   VGAUND  .FRS    4,096  05-31-91 12:00p
  VIDEO7  .VRS     8,131  05-31-91 12:00p   VIKING  .VRS   36,779  03-30-90 12:00p
  WDPERF5 .LOD    10,240  11-06-89 10:43a   WIN30-WP.PIF      545  01-22-91 11:51p
  WP      .DRS   490,022  05-31-91 12:00p   WP      .FIL  617,336  05-31-91 12:00p
  WP      .LRS    25,051  05-31-91 12:00p   WP      .MRS    6,072  05-31-91 12:00p
  WP      .PIF       545  05-31-91 12:00p   WP      .QRS   17,034  05-31-91 12:00p
  WP{WP}  .SET     5,597  07-08-91 11:22a   WP{WP}US.LCM       16  11-16-89 12:06p
  WP}WP{  .BV1         0  07-10-91 02:10p   WP}WP{  .CHK        0  07-10-91 02:10p
  WP}WP{  .SPC     4,096  07-10-91 02:10p ▼ WP}WP{  .TV1        0  07-10-91 02:10p

 letter.1                              (Name Search; Enter or arrows to Exit)
```

6. You will be returned to the main editing window. If the main editing screen was empty, the name of the document will appear on the status line. If you retrieved another document into a document you were already editing, the file name won't change (or if no name was previously given, there will still be no file name until you save the document).

Moving the cursor

As you know, the little flashing line or block that you see on your screen is the cursor. The cursor's location is where the action takes place! This section teaches you how to move the cursor around the page for editing. There are two simple rules to remember:

✻ You can't move the cursor to a place where you have never typed. In the example given in the section "Entering Text," you can't move the cursor past the word *Jane*.

✻ Although you *can* move the cursor with the arrow keys, there are almost always faster ways. If you learn the shortcuts, you'll save a lot of time.

There are many time-saving shortcuts for moving the cursor around the WordPerfect screen.

Moving the Cursor with the Arrow Keys

You have two basic ways to move the cursor with the arrow keys so that it's where you want it. Use the up or down arrow to move the cursor up one line or down one line at a time. (If you are at the top of the letter, you won't be able to move up any farther. If you are at the bottom of the letter, you won't be able to move down any farther.) Press the left or right arrow once to move the cursor left one character or right one character at a time.

Go ahead and try it. Move around the document by pressing the arrow keys. Now try holding down one of the arrow keys constantly.

You probably notice that when an arrow key is held down, the cursor moves quickly. Because the cursor zips right along, holding down an arrow key to get quickly from one part of the letter to another is possible, but it's not really the best way.

Why? Because you can't stop the cursor on a dime when it is moving quickly. By the time you let go of an arrow key, either the cursor has not gone far enough, or it has gone too far. So you end up having to jockey back and forth to get the cursor where you want it. This is a major time waster! So the rule is this: use the arrow keys only if you are moving the cursor a very short distance.

I'm showing you this because the natural tendency is to use the arrow keys to move the cursor around . Now that you know that this isn't the best way to move around a letter, you will appreciate the next section even more.

Moving the cursor the easy way

WordPerfect offers a number of special key combinations that move the cursor quickly and accurately around a letter. These movements fall into a couple of simple categories, listed in the following table.

The first column tells you where you want to go. The second column tells you what key (or keys) to press to get there. For key combinations that contain a comma, such as *Home, up arrow*, press the first key and then the second. For key combinations that contain a hyphen, such as *Ctrl-up arrow* , press and hold down the first key, and while that key is still pressed, press the second key.

Moving along the line

End of line	End
Beginning of line	Home, Home, left arrow
One word to the left	Ctrl-left arrow
One word to the right	Ctrl-right arrow

Moving around the page

One paragraph up	Ctrl-up arrow
One paragraph down	Ctrl-down arrow
Bottom of the screen	Plus key (numeric keypad)
Top of the screen	Minus key (numeric keypad)
Top of the current page	Home, up arrow
Bottom of the current page	Home, down arrow
Beginning of letter	Home, Home, up arrow
End of letter	Home, Home, down arrow

With the sample letter on the screen, use each one of these shortcut keystroke combinations. When you begin using Word-Perfect for your own letters, keep this book open to this page for easy reference. Don't get in the habit of using the arrow keys to move around your document. Once you learn these 12 combinations, you will save yourself a lot of time and effort. After a few hours of using them, they will become atuomatic.

If you get into the bad habit of using just the arrow keys for movement, you'll never learn this faster way of doing things. So spend the time learning these special key combinations as you learn WordPerfect, and you'll find word processing much more enjoyable.

The rule of thumb for making sure that you've moved the cursor in front of any hidden codes (see Chapter 2) is to press the Home key one extra time. For example, Home, Home, up arrow moves you to the beginning of the document, placing the cursor in front of any codes. Home, Home, Home, left arrow moves you to the beginning of a line, placing the cursor in front of any codes.

Using the mouse to move the cursor

If you have a mouse, you can use it to easily insert the cursor anywhere on the screen.

Whenever you move the mouse, an unblinking block cursor is visible (this block cursor disappears as soon as you begin typing). To insert the cursor anywhere on the screen, move the mouse block cursor to where you want and click on the left mouse button. (Note: With some monitors, the mouse cursor is shaped like an arrow.) If you click the right mouse button, the menu bar is activated. To deactivate the menu bar, press the right mouse button a second time.

Notes

_____

_____

_____

_____

_____

_____

_____

_____

_____

_____

_____

Editing text

Editing text with a word processor involves one of three things:

Cut! Paste! Move! That's editing in a "nutshell."

* Deleting (erasing) text. Deleting text means getting rid of text you don't want. You might want to delete anything from a single character or word to a paragraph or even many pages.

* Inserting (adding) text. Inserting text means placing additional text either in the middle of text you have already typed or at the beginning or end of the letter. You can insert anything from a single character or word to a paragraph or even many pages.

* Moving text. Moving text means relocating text that you have already typed. This activity might involve moving a word, sentence, paragraph, or page from one place in your letter to another. You may also want to insert text from an already written letter into the letter you are currently writing. Moving text is discussed in detail in Chapter 7.

Deleting text

You can delete a letter, a word, a paragraph, or a page with just a few keystrokes. Most of the following explanations of how to delete text contain examples that you can use on the sample text.

Deleting a Single Character

To delete a single character, place the cursor to the right of the character and press Backspace. Or place the cursor under a character and press Delete.

In the sample text, position the cursor under the second *i* in *liiving*. Press Delete. Note that the second *i* disappears.

Deleting a Single Word

Place the cursor under the word and press Delete Word (Ctrl-Backspace).

In the sample text, position the cursor under the first *room*. Press Ctrl-Backspace.

Deleting a Single Sentence

Place the cursor in the sentence. Press Move (Ctrl-F4) and choose **1 S**entence then choose **3 D**elete.

In the sample text, position the cursor anywhere in the sentence that begins *We'll hold you to your promise....* Press Move (Ctrl-F4) and choose **1 S**entence (the entire sentence will be highlighted) then choose **3 D**elete.

Deleting a Single Paragraph

Place the cursor in the paragraph. Press Move (Ctrl-F4), choose **2 P**aragraph, and then choose **3 D**elete.

In the sample text, position the cursor anywhere in the paragraph that begins *Would you please ask him....* Press

Move (Ctrl-F4), choose **2 P**aragraph (the entire paragraph will be highlighted), and then choose **3 D**elete.

Deleting a Single Page

Place the cursor in a sentence that's on the page you want to delete. Press Move (Ctrl-F4), choose **3 P**age, and then choose **3 D**elete.

Deleting a Single Line

Pressing Delete to End of Line (Ctrl-End) deletes all the text from the right of the cursor to the end of the line.

In the sample text, place the cursor anywhere in the sentence that begins *It was great you and Jeff...* and press Delete to End of Line (Ctrl-End). All the text to the right of the cursor to the end of the line will be deleted.

If you place the cursor at the beginning of the line, pressing Ctrl-End will delete the entire line of text.

Deleting the Rest of the Page

Pressing Delete to the End of the Page (Ctrl-PgDn), and then confirming with **Y**es, deletes all the text from the right of the cursor to the end of the current page.

Deleting Backward

Place the cursor in the appropriate word. Press Home, Backspace to delete the part of the word left of the cursor.

In the sample text, place the cursor on the *r* in *Yours* in the closing. Press Home and then press Backspace. The letters *You* will be deleted.

Deleting Forward

Place the cursor in the appropriate word. Press Home, Delete to delete the part of the word above and to the right of the cursor.

In the sample text, place the cursor on the *u* in *truly* in the closing. Press Home and then press Delete. The letters *uly* will be deleted.

Deleting Blocked Text

Place the cursor at the beginning of the block of text you want to delete. Press Block (Alt-F4). Using the arrow keys (or other movement keys), move the cursor to the end of the block you want to delete. (If you are using the mouse, you can select a block of text by clicking and dragging across the page.) Press Delete. Press Y when you see the prompt Delete Block? **N**o (**Y**es). (More on deleting blocks of text is found in Chapter 7.)

Place the cursor under the *J* in *June* in the date. Press Block (Alt-F4). Using the cursor arrow keys, expand the block by moving the cursor to the end of the salutation. Press Delete. Press Y when you see the prompt Delete Block? **N**o (**Y**es). The date and salutation will be deleted.

Notes

Undeleting text

With all this deleting power, at some point you will either accidentally delete some text or else change your mind and wish you hadn't deleted something. Fortunately, WordPerfect is very forgiving and will let you "undo" any of the last three deletions you have made.

Whoops! Cut something you didn't mean to cut? Use Undelete to get it back.

To "undelete" text, do the following:

1. Press Cancel (F1)

or

Choose **U**ndelete from the **E**dit menu.

2. Your last deletion reappears highlighted on the screen. It is not yet undeleted, however. You must tell WordPerfect to restore the deletion. At the bottom of the screen you'll see this menu:

Undelete: 1 Restore **2 P**revious Deletion: **0**

To restore the text, select **1 R**estore. If the current highlighted deletion isn't the one you want restored, you can look at the last three deletions by selecting **2 P**revious Deletion (you can also use the up or down arrow to cycle through the three deletions). Once the deletion you want is on-screen, select **1 R**estore.

Note: If the deleted text contains any hidden codes, they will be restored along with any text you undelete. Depending on your system, WordPerfect may run out of space when trying to save long deletions in the Undelete area of its memory. If this happens, WordPerfect will warn you and ask you to confirm whether you really want to complete the deletion.

To practice undeleting, do the following:

1. Place the cursor under the word *Dear* in the salutation.

2. Press Ctrl-Delete to delete the word.

3. Press Cancel (F1)

or

Choose **U**ndelete from the **E**dit menu.

4. The deleted word *Dear* appears in a block on the screen (see fig. 3.3). It is not really undeleted yet. You will see the following prompt:

Undelete: 1 Restore; **2 P**revious Deletion: **0**

To complete the undeletion, select 1 Restore. The word *Dear* is now undeleted.

Fig. 3.3.

The word *Dear* being undeleted.

```
June 16, 1991

Dear Mitch,

It was great you and Jeff could come up for the weekend. We enjoyed your company
The only problem is the visit was too short.

We reelly liked Jeff's ideas about the liiving room room. After his explanation,
became clear that the fireplace should be the focal point of the living room. In
to do that, we now need to look for two new sofas instead of one!

Our old house finally sold, so we will soon have the money to work with for
purchasing new living room furniture.

Would you please ask him if he thinks we should try and get the furniture to mat
the carpet or consider an Oriental rug and then try and match the furniture to i
refresh his memory, we had looked at pattern H7122.

We'll hold you to your promise to visit again before the end of summer.

Yours truly,


Undelete: 1 Restore; 2 Previous Deletion: 0
```

Inserting text

When you use a typewriter, if you type where something is already typed, the new letter is typed on top of the old letter, overprinting it and making it hard to read.

When you type with WordPerfect, if the cursor is under a letter you have already typed, the newly typed letter takes up the space where the old letter was, and the old letter marches one step to the right. This process is called *insertion*.

Try inserting text into the sample letter:

1. Move the cursor (using keyboard shortcuts if you can) to the letter *p* in the word *pattern* in the fourth paragraph.

2. To insert a new word, type *carpet* and then press the space bar once. The word *carpet* has been inserted just before the word *pattern*.

3. Now move the cursor to the space just after the word *match* in the first sentence of the fourth paragraph.

4. Press the space bar once and then type the phrase *the color of*. Did you see the entire line of text move to the right to accommodate the new word? (You may notice letters going off the right edge of screen. Don't worry. As soon as you move the cursor anywhere, the words will "wrap" correctly to the new line.)

Note: If any hidden codes are after the insertion point, they will also be pushed ahead of any characters you insert.

Forget a word, sentence, or even a paragraph? WordPerfect lets you insert whatever you forgot.

Typing over text

Want WordPerfect to behave more like a typewriter?

Use the Typeover feature.

With a word processor, the default setting is "insertion on." That is, when you place a cursor in the middle of text and begin typing, the new text is inserted rather than writing over the existing text. If you are used to a typewriter, you may sometimes feel more comfortable typing over existing text–having new text take the place of old text instead of just having new text shove old text along ahead.

In WordPerfect, the process of replacing letters as you type is called *typeover*. You can make WordPerfect type over existing text by pressing the Insert key. When you press the Insert key, the word `Typeover` appears on the left-hand side of the status line. To return to insertion, press the Insert key again, and the word `Typeover` disappears.

You will find that using Insert and then deleting any extra words or characters is more efficient than using the Typeover feature regularly. If you use Typeover, you must press the Insert key frequently to toggle back and forth between Typeover and Insert. You may also accidentally leave Typeover active and end up replacing something you didn't mean to. So although WordPerfect offers the Typeover feature, you're usually better off not using it.

To practice using the Typeover feature, do the following:

1. Place the cursor under the *J* in *June* in the date.

2. Press Insert (the word `Typeover` should appear on the status line).

3. Type *July*. Notice that the word *June* doesn't move to the right–the letters you type just replace the letters in the word *June*. Because the first two letters in June and July are the same, you won't notice any changes until you replace *ne* with *ly*.

Note: If there are any hidden codes after the cursor, those codes will be pushed ahead of any characters you type. In other words, you don't end up typing over codes. Also, while Typeover is on, the Tab key doesn't insert a tab it only moves the cursor to the next tab stop. In addition, the space bar doesn't insert a space but instead replaces the character above the cursor with a space.

Another Typeover quirk: The letters you type over are treated by WordPerfect as if you'd deleted them, so you can use the Undelete feature to restore text you accidentally type over.

Using the thesaurus

Never be stuck for the right word again.

Use WordPerfect's built-in thesaurus to expand your vocabulary.

A thesaurus is a compilation of synonyms–that is, words that mean similar things. For example, imagine that you are writing to a prospective customer and want to describe the type of service your company offers. After typing the phrase *excellent service*, you begin to wonder whether you couldn't phrase it better.

This is where the thesaurus comes in. Looking up *excellent*, you are led to *superior* and then led to *exceptional*, *extraordinary*, *outstanding*, and *phenomenal*, to name a few of the synonyms supplied by WordPerfect. Any of these words might better describe the type of service you want the customer to understand your company offers. All pack more of a punch than the often used *excellent*.

By using a thesaurus, writers can choose (pick, select, specify) exactly the right word. Secretaries and business people can use a thesaurus to help their letters sound clearer or more interesting. By having an electronic assistant always at your fingertips, you can improve your writing while you expand your vocabulary.

To practice using the WordPerfect thesaurus on the sample letter, do the following:

1. Place the cursor anywhere under the word *problem* in the first paragraph.

2. Press Thesaurus (Alt-F1)

or

Choose **T**hesaurus from the **T**ools menu.

Your document screen will split in two (see fig. 3.4). The

top part of the screen shows the word *problem* highlighted. The bottom part of the screen is the thesaurus. It is split into three columns where the synonyms for your word are displayed. In this example, there are words to take up one and a half columns.

Fig. 3.4

The WordPerfect thesaurus.

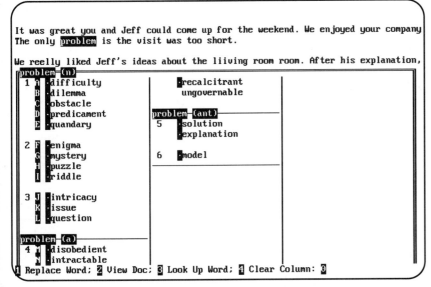

At the top of the left column is your word, called a *headword*. The rest of the words are either synonyms (words that mean something similar to the headword) or antonyms (words that mean the opposite of the headword). Some listings for headwords break down the synonyms into categories of nouns (n), adjectives (a), or verbs (v). (The word *antonyms* is abbreviated "ant" by WordPerfect. Not all headwords have antonyms.)

Words in the list that are preceded by a bullet are headwords in their own right and have their own synonyms and antonyms. If a word isn't preceded by a bullet, it's not a headword.

In the example, all the words except *ungovernable* are also headwords (*ungovernable* isn't preceded by a bullet).

You will also notice that some of the synonyms are grouped together. WordPerfect's thesaurus groups words with common meanings, making it easier to select the best word. For example, in group 2, the words *enigma, mystery, puzzle*, and *riddle* are grouped because they all have a similar meaning. Synonyms for *problem* in the sample letter are in group 1.

In the first column, all the words are preceded by a letter of the alphabet. This letter can be used in two different ways:

✱ If you press the letter next to a headword (for example, press A, which is next to the word *difficulty*), then in one of the adjacent columns up pops the word as its own headword with its synonyms and antonyms. If you want see synonyms for yet another headword, press a corresponding letter. You may have noticed that there are alphabetical letters in only one column at a time. If you want to shift the alphabetical letters from one column to the next, press the right or left arrow to rotate among the lists. (The up and down arrows can be used to scroll the list in a single column.)

✱ If you select **1** (Replace Word), you are prompted `Press letter for word`. Press the alphabetical letter that corresponds to the word you want to substitute for your selected word, and *voilà*: the thesaurus disappears, and your word is replaced. For example, if you press **1** (Replace Word) and then press A (for *difficulty*), the word *difficulty* will replace *problem*.

The other choices available from the status-line menu are these:

1 `Replace Word` **2** `View Doc` **3** `Look Up Word` **4** `Clear Column:` **0**

The first choice was just explained. If you choose **2** (View Doc), you can scroll through your document until you press Exit (F7) and return to the thesaurus.

If you select **3** (Look Up Word), you can type another word for the thesaurus to look up. If you choose **4** (Clear Column), the selected column where the alphabetical letters are will disappear. You can use this feature to clear space to look at more headwords.

Try out the different menu choices to see how they work. With some experimentation, you'll discover how you can take a single word and examine various meanings until you find the right word for your document.

After finishing this chapter, save the letter again as LETTER.1.

You will be using LETTER.1 again in Chapter 6.

Chapter 4: Setting margins

In Chapter 3, you learned how to create, save, and retrieve a WordPerfect document. You also learned various ways to navigate through the editing screen. By the end of the chapter, you were familiar with various editing commands and ways to delete and undelete text. In other words, you learned how to control what the text should *say*.

In the next two chapters, you'll learn how to control how the text should *look*.

In this chapter, you learn how to change margin settings. You will also learn how to center a letter on a page. Finally, you'll learn how to modify WordPerfect's settings to accommodate pre-printed letterhead or stationery.

Basic style and margin settings are the underpinnings of a document's format.

This chapter shows you how to control margins.

Putting your best foot forward

A letter or report is more than just words: it is an image presented by you or your company to the rest of the world. Although what you *say* is important, how the document *looks* may make the difference between its being taken seriously or ending up in the trash.

Depending on your job, you may have different considerations about a document's appearance. The following is a list of questions to consider before you send your document out into the world. The rest of this chapter discusses how you can use WordPerfect to make your documents look the way you want them to.

✻ **If you are a secretary,** how should the document look? Does the company have style guidelines for correspondence or reports?

✻ **If you are an executive,** does your organization have style guidelines? Have you implemented them? Do your secretarial associates follow them?

✻ **If you are an entrepreneur or new business owner,** what look do you want your documents to have? What kind of image are you trying to project?

✻ **If you are a student,** what look should your report or paper have? How can you gain an edge over your fellow students with reports that look particularly sharp?

Understanding design considerations

Because the appearance of a document depends in large part on its physical design–how the words look on the page–you should take into account many design considerations:

Have you ever thought what the physical appearance of your correspondence says about you or your company?

✳ **Stationery or paper.** What kind, color, and weight of paper are you using? Is the paper plain, pre-printed, or embossed with your company's logo and letterhead?

✳ **Font choice.** Does your company have a corporate font (typeface)? Or are you limited to the choices your printer offers?

✳ **Margins and white space.** What margins (top, bottom, left, and right) will you use? If you have a short letter, do you center it on the page?

✳ **Paragraph style.** Do you double-space between paragraphs? Do you indent the first line of each paragraph? Do you have fully justified or left-justified paragraphs?

✳ **Letter style.** Will you be using the block, modified block, modified semi-block, hanging indent, or simplified letter styles? (See the next section for some explanation of these styles.)

✳ **Letter elements.** How will different letter elements such as the date, salutation, address, body, closing, signature, typist's initials, and other information be formatted?

Although this book won't tell you what style to use for your letter or report, the rest of this chapter explains how to modify WordPerfect so that whatever you decide can be implemented.

Understanding margins

Space from the edge of the paper is the "margin."

Change the way your letter looks by setting different margins, advancing or centering a page–all with a few simple commands.

When you use WordPerfect, the default margins are electronically preset before you even begin typing. The preset margins are 1 inch all around (top, bottom, left, and right). For many people, these margins are just fine. However, you may want different margins.

Here are some guidelines for using margins:

✳ **If you are using plain paper** that doesn't have anything pre-printed on it, you probably don't need to change the margins.

✳ **If you are using company stationery** that has a letterhead or logo, you may need to change the margins to prevent WordPerfect from printing on top of pre-printed items. To see if changes are needed, take a sheet of the stationery or letterhead and make a mark where you want printing to begin. For example, if your letterhead includes a logo and address that extend 2 inches from the top of the page, you'll want the printing to start below the pre-printed information.

Some stationery or letterhead may also require changes in the left or bottom margins also.

Use the sample letter LETTER.1 to practice making margin changes. If the document isn't already on-screen, retrieve it using the commands you learned in Chapter 3.

Margin changes aren't always readily apparent on the screen unless they are extreme. To see the effect of margin changes, you usually need to view or print the document (see below or Chapter 6). Also, page breaks (the end of one page and the start of another) are represented in the main editing screen by a dotted line that extends all the way from the left to the right of your screen.

Changing top and bottom margins

WordPerfect comes with default top and bottom margins of 1 inch. If you want different margins in order to accommodate your stationery, you'll first need to measure from the top and bottom edges of the paper to where you want the margins to begin.

Using the sample letter to change margins, perform the following steps (in this example, you'll change the top and bottom margins to 2 inches each; the margins you'll actually use in your work may be different):

1. Move the cursor to the beginning of the document (press Home, Home, up arrow).

2. Press Format (Shift-F8) and select **2** - **P**age

or

Choose **P**age from the **L**ayout menu. (See figure 4.1.)

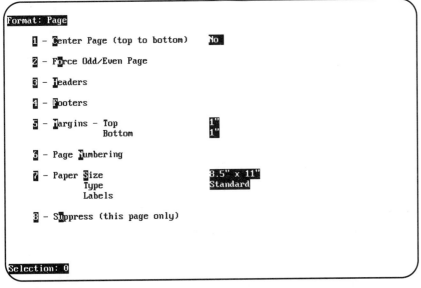

Fig. 4.1.

The Format: Page menu.

3. Choose **5** - **M**argins.

4. Type *2*" for the top margin and press Enter. Type *2*" for the bottom margin and press Enter. (Type the " mark or the letter *i*–for inch–so that WordPerfect will interpret the new margin number in inches.) Notice that the status line now says Ln 2".

5. Press Exit (F7) to return to the main editing screen of WordPerfect.

Using the Advance feature

After you change the top and bottom margins, WordPerfect inserts a **[T/B Mar]** code into your document. This code affects all pages that follow, so you must make sure to place the code at the top of the first page you want to affect.

If you are making a margin change to accommodate stationary or letterhead, you most likely will want the default 1" margins restored after the first page–because most companies use letterhead only on the initial page, and regular stationery on subsequent pages. If so, remember to change the margins back at the top of the second page of your letter.

Another option is to use WordPerfect's Advance feature.

WordPerfect's Advance feature lets you "skip" to the part of the page you want to begin printing. For example, to force the sample letter to begin printing 3 inches from the top of the page, do the following:

1. Move to the beginning of the letter (by pressing Home, Home, up arrow).

2. Press Format (Shift-F8) and choose **4** - **O**ther

or

Choose **O**ther from the **L**ayout menu.

3. Choose **1** - **A**dvance.

4. Then choose **3** - Line.

5. At the Adv. to line prompt, type *3* " and press Enter.

6. Press Exit (F7) to return to the main editing screen.

WordPerfect inserts an **[AdvToLn]** code into the document. You cannot see this advance on the editing screen. You can, however, see the advance when you preview or print the document, which you'll do in Chapter 6. Previewing is briefly described in the next section.

Previewing a document

A reminder: Unless you change the margins radically so that an entire page fits on your 25-line screen, you won't see on-screen the changes in the top and bottom margins. To see the changes, you can print or preview the document.

While previewing will be described more fully in Chapter 6, you can see a graphic representation of the page by doing the following:

1. Press Print (Shift-F7)

or

Choose **P**rint from the **F**ile menu.

2. Choose **6 - V**iew Document.

After you have finished previewing, you can return to the main editing screen, by pressing Exit (F7).

Changing left and right margins

WordPerfect comes with default left and right margins of 1 inch. If you want different margins in order to accommodate your stationery, you'll first need to measure from the left and right edges of the paper to where you want the margins to begin.

Because changing left and right margins uses almost exactly the same steps as changing top and bottom margins, what follows may sound familiar. Using the sample letter to change margins, perform the following steps (In this example, you'll change the left margin to 2 inches and the right margin to 1.5 inches; the margins you'll actually use in your work may be different):

1. Move the cursor to the beginning of the document (press Home, Home, up arrow).

2. Press Format (Shift-F8) and choose **1 - L**ine

or

Choose **L**ine from the **L**ayout menu. (See figure 4.2.)

3. Choose **7 - M**argins.

4. Type *2*" for the left margin and press Enter. Type *1.5*" for the right margin and press Enter. (Type the " mark or the letter *i*–for inch–so that WordPerfect will interpret the new margin number in inches.) Notice that the status line now says Pos 2".

5. Press Exit (F7) to return to the main editing screen of WordPerfect.

```
Format: Line
      1 - Hyphenation                        No
      2 - Hyphenation Zone - Left           10%
                            Right            4%
      3 - Justification                     Left
      4 - Line Height                       Auto
      5 - Line Numbering                    No
      6 - Line Spacing                      1
      7 - Margins - Left                    1"
                    Right                   1"
      8 - Tab Set                           Rel; -1", every 0.5"
      9 - Widow/Orphan Protection           No


Selection: 0
```

Fig. 4.2.

The Format: Line menu.

Note: Depending on how much you narrow the margins, you may not see the changes in left and right margins on-screen. With the margin change you just made, there will probably be a noticeable narrowing of the line of text. (If you want to preview the document, follow the steps described in the previous section or see Chapter 6.)

After you perform these steps, WordPerfect inserts a **[L/R Mar]** code into your document. This code affects all text that follows, until the end of the document or until another margin code is encountered. If you need to, you can change left and right margins just for part of your document. Just set the margins at the point you want the changes to take place. Then, after you are done typing the material you want to appear with different margins, do the above steps again, but reset the margins to their original values.

Centering a letter on a page

Some documents, like a short letter or a memo of only a paragraph or two, fill only part of the page. When you print very short documents and only the top half of the paper is filled, the document looks odd (see fig. 4.3).

You can tell WordPerfect to print short letters or memos so that they are physically centered top to bottom on the paper (see fig. 4.4). Obviously, this feature overrides your top

```
                    Schuyler W. Lininger, Jr., D.C.
                           PO Box 86832
                         Portland, OR 97286

        August 12, 1991

        Dear Marcia,

        It was nice meeting you last week. I appreciate the time you were able to
        spend talking about our products.

        The number of products I'm suggesting will fill one shelf plus a few
        bottles. The reason for the extras is that you now put a few items, like
        lecithin, on a separate shelf. One reason for sending all the samples is
        so you can verify what will fit on the shelf.

        I look forward to working with you in providing quality products to your
        customers, in providing educational presentations to your staff, and in
        creating literature that you can use in educating your customers and staff.

        Yours truly,


        Skye Lininger, D.C.
        Vice-President, Sales
```

Fig. 4.3.

**A short letter that is not
centered from top to
bottom**

and bottom margin settings.

To center the sample letter vertically, do the following:

1. Move the cursor to the top of the document (press Home, Home, up arrow).

2. Press Format (Shift-F8) and choose **2 - P**age

or

Choose **P**age from the **L**ayout menu.

3. Choose **1 - C**enter Page (top to bottom).

4. Press Y (for Yes).

Schuyler W. Lininger, Jr., D.C.
PO Box 86832
Portland, OR 97286

August 12, 1991

Dear Marcia,

It was nice meeting you last week. I appreciate the time you were able to
spend talking about our products.

The number of products I'm suggesting will fill one shelf plus a few
bottles. The reason for the extras is that you now put a few items, like
lecithin, on a separate shelf. One reason for sending all the samples is
so you can verify what will fit on the shelf.

I look forward to working with you in providing quality products to your
customers, in providing educational presentations to your staff, and in
creating literature that you can use in educating your customers and staff.

Yours truly,

Skye Lininger, D.C.
Vice-President, Sales

Fig. 4.4.

A short letter centered from top to bottom.

5. Press Exit (F7) to return to the main editing screen.

When you print or preview the document (see above or Chapter 6), it will print with the text vertically centered on the page.

If you are using pre-printed stationery, you may not want to use this feature, because the result may not look very attractive. But don't be afraid of experimenting.

Chapter 5: Changing the appearance of text

In the last chapter, you learned how to set and change margins–which affects the overall way a document looks. In this chapter, you'll learn how to change the appearance of the text itself.

You'll learn how to change the font; bold and underline text; control alignment (justification, centering, and tabs); and use indents and margin release.

If you are new to word processing, the things you'll learn in this chapter will amaze and delight you. You'll gain a sense of control over the letter or report you are creating. Depending on your printer, you'll be able to change or emphasize

Text handling is the essence of this chapter. You'll learn about fonts and how to affect their appearance.

5|82

fonts to call attention to particular words, phrases, or sections of your document. Using alignment controls, you'll be able to create tabular reports–with columns of information properly lining up.

After this chapter, you're in the home stretch and ready for Chapter 6 where you'll spell-check and print your letter.

Notes

_____

_____

_____

_____

_____

_____

_____

_____

_____

_____

_____

_____

Understanding the base font

With a typewriter you're fairly limited as to how the type will look on a page. On some typewriters you can change type balls or wheels for variety, but that capability doesn't touch the number of ways WordPerfect enables you to change the way type looks.

Think of the base font as the font the document would automatically print in if you didn't make any changes at all.

WordPerfect uses some specific terms that relate to "type." Here are two you need to know now:

✳ **Font** is a typeface of a particular point size (size) and appearance. The fonts available to you depend mostly on what kind of printer you have.

✳ **Point size** is a rough measure of the vertical height of a font. There are 72 points to an inch, so a 36-point font is about a half-inch high. Most letters (documents, not alphabetical characters) are set in 12-point type. Some printers–especially dot-matrix ones–don't use point sizes for measuring. If you use a laser printer, you will probably specify point size. See figure 5.1 for examples of different point sizes.

✳ **Typeface** is a particular letter design. Some typefaces have small strokes that come off the end of each letter (the strokes are called serifs); some typefaces don't have any finishing strokes (those typefaces are called sans serif); and some typefaces are decorative (called display fonts) and used only for impact in headlines or advertising.

When you installed your printer (either during the initial installation of WordPerfect or when you added a new printer),

12 point

18 point

36 point

48 point

72 point

Fig. 5.1.

Text set in different point sizes.

a font and point size (together called the *Base Font* was automatically selected by WordPerfect.

Understanding Factors that Affect the Base Font

WordPerfect lets you change the initial base font (the default font) in several ways. This chapter will only discuss how to change a font by inserting a hidden code–the other methods are described in Appendix A.

The fonts you can choose are based on four things:

✳ **Built-in fonts** are fonts your printer comes with. WordPerfect knows all about these fonts and gives you access to them.

✳ **Downloadable and cartridge fonts** are fonts that are not built in to your printer but that can be used by your printer. If these fonts are already installed, you can use them. A discussion of how to install these kinds of fonts is too complicated for this book. If you need help with this topic, refer to your WordPerfect manual.

✳ **Your printer's selection of point sizes for each font.** Some printers (most notably PostScript and Hewlett-Packard Laser Jet III) have "scalable" fonts. These printers let you set a wide range of point sizes.

✳ Whether you want landscape or portrait orientation, which some printers offer particular fonts for. (Landscape is the long way on a page; portrait is the "normal," or short, way.) Depending on how you have your paper set to print (see Chapter 6), you may need to choose landscape or portrait fonts. Almost all letters and reports are printed the short way, in portrait orientation.

Notes

_____

_____

_____

_____

_____

_____

_____

_____

_____

_____

_____

_____

_____

5|86 Changing the base font

When you insert a [Font] hidden code, the base font changes from that point on in your document.

To have a document to work on in this chapter, from a clean screen, type in the following text and save as LETTER.2.

```
June 25, 1991

Dear Mr. Jones,

It was a pleasure meeting you yesterday. I was delighted to hear you might
be opening a new health food store. I was also pleased to hear you are
considering featuring our line of nutritional supplements.

As we discussed, here are some discounts we can offer:

Opening Order Second Order Third Order

15% 10% 5%

Here is what the total would be over a period of three months with the
suggested inventory:

First Month 1,000.00
Second Month 550.00
Third Month 400.00

Total 1,950.00

We look forward to a warm and mutually beneficial relationship.

Yours truly,


Skye Lininger
Vice President, Sales
```

Fig 5.2

The sample LETTER.2.

To change the base font, do the following:

1. Go to the beginning of the document (press Home, Home, Up Arrow). Press Font (Ctrl-F8) and choose **4** - Base **F**ont

or

Choose Base **F**ont from the **F**ont menu.

2. From the list, use the arrow keys to scroll up and down until you find the font you want. (If you're not sure what font to change to, you can reselect the current base font–the font with the asterisk next to it.)

3. Choose **1 S**elect or press Enter. Some printers ask you for a point size. If yours does, type a point size–12 is good for most letters and reports–and press Exit (F7) or Enter.

These steps insert the hidden formatting code **[Font:*Font <point size>*]**. (Not all printer fonts have a point size included, so don't be concerned if the hidden code you insert isn't followed by a point size.)

This hidden code changes the base font from the point where the code is inserted until the end of the document or until another hidden font code is encountered.

5|88 Changing the appearance of text

The appearance of a font refers to "text effects" like bold, underline, and italics.

Appearance, as defined by WordPerfect, refers to particular characteristics of the way a font looks. In specifying a font's appearance, you can choose among bold, underline, double-underline, italic, outline, shadow, small capital letters, redline, and strikeout.

What some of these appearances end up looking like will vary depending on the type of printer you have. See figure 5.3 for examples.

Fig. 5.3.

Examples of some of the different text appearances.

Bold

<u>Underline</u>

Italic

Outline

Shadow

~~Strikeout~~

For the greatest impact, use appearance attributes sparingly. Because a typewriter usually limits you to underlining (and sometimes bold), in typing that effect gets overused. With a word processor, you rarely use underlined text. Some people use bold text for emphasis, but bold text "shouts" from the page and should be used sparingly. For book titles or emphasis, use italics.

If you want to see what each appearance attribute looks like on your printer, print out the document PRINTER.TST (see next section).

To change the text's appearance, do the following:

1. Move to the top of the document (Home, Home, Up Arrow) and press Enter. This inserts a line before the date. Move the cursor up to the blank line.

2. Press Font (Ctrl-F8) and choose **2 A**ppearance

or

Choose **A**ppearance from the F**o**nt menu.

3. If you used the Font (Ctrl-F8) key, you will see this status-line menu:

1 Bold **2 U**ndln **3 D**bl Und **4 I**talc **5 O**utln **6** Shadw **7** Sm **C**ap **8 R**edln **9 S**tkout: **0**

or

If you used the pull-down menus, you will see a pop-out menu listing the nine appearance choices.

You can choose any one of the nine appearance choices, but for this example, choose **6** Sh**a**dw (status line) or Sh**a**dow (pop-out).

WordPerfect inserts a pair of hidden codes into your document. In this example, a pair of **[SHADW][shadw]** codes is inserted. Your cursor is actually positioned *between* the uppercase "ON" code and the lowercase "off" code. Whatever you type will be in shadow until you move the cursor beyond the "off" code.

4. Type the name of the company: *Sunshine Northwest, Inc.*

5. To turn off the appearance code, press Font (Ctrl-F8) and choose **3 N**ormal

or

Choose **N**ormal from the **F**o**n**t menu.

Note: These menu choices move the cursor past the "off" code. Once you understand this, if you want, you can save a few keystrokes by using the right arrow to move the cursor past the "off" code.

Depending on your monitor, the text with the new appearance may or may not look different on-screen. You may have to print or preview the document to see the effect. (Also, not all printers show the shadow appearance.)

Notes

_____

_____

_____

_____

_____

_____

_____

_____

_____

_____

_____

Printing the printer test file

WordPerfect provides a file called PRINTER.TST (found in the WP51 directory). When you print this file, you can test many of the capabilities of your particular printer. To print this document, do the following:

1. Press Retrieve (Shift-F10)

or

Choose **R**etrieve from the **F**ile menu.

2. Type *C:\WP51\PRINTER.TST* and press Enter. (Note that your drive and directory may be different.)

or

Use the List (F5) feature to locate and retrieve the PRINTER.TST document.

3. Press Print (Shift-F7)

or

Choose **P**rint from the **F**ile menu.

4. Choose **1** - **F**ull Document.

To see what your printer is capable of, print the PRINTER.TST document.

It features almost every effect WordPerfect is capable of.

5|92 Bolding and underlining text

Remember F6 for Bold and F8 for Underline.

Because the bold and underline appearance attributes are commonly used, WordPerfect has given each of these functions its own key.

You will save time and effort by boldfacing or underlining your text by using the Bold (F6) or Underline (F8) key instead of the menu steps previously described.

Press Bold (F6) or Underline (F8) once to turn "on" the effect; press the same key a second time to turn "off" the effect.

You can mix appearance styles. For example, text can be *both* **<u>bold and underlined</u>**.

Changing the size of text

Size, as defined by WordPerfect, is related to but different from point size. You can set relative sizes from the Font menu. Sizes offered are superscript, subscript, fine, small, large, very large, and extra large. (WordPerfect calculates these sizes as a percentage of the base font.)

Not all printers can handle font size changes.

Most dot-matrix and all PostScript printers have this capability.

You can affect the size of a font by making it superscript, subscript, fine, small, large, very large, and extra large. The sizes that actually print depend mostly on what kind of printer you have. See figure 5.4 for examples of size changes.

Normal ^{superscript}

Normal _{subscript}

Fine

Small

Large

Very Large

Extra Large

Fig. 5.4.

Examples of size changes.

These size changes should not be used except when war-ranted. For example, superscripts are useful for footnotes or endnotes; subscripts are useful for some scientific references; size changes can sometimes be used for emphasis in headings.

To change font size in the sample letter, do the following:

1. Move the cursor to end of the line that contains the name of the company (*Sunshine Northwest, Inc.*) and press Enter.

2. Press Font (Ctrl-F8) and choose **1 S**ize

or

Choose the F**o**nt menu.

3. If you used the Font (Ctrl-F8) key, you will see this status-line menu:

1 Su**p**rscpt; **2** Su**b**scpt; **3 F**ine; **4 S**mall; **5 L**arge; **6 V**ry Large; **7 E**xt Large: **0**

or

If you used the pull-down menus, you will see the seven size choices listed on the menu.

You can select any of the seven choices. For this example, choose **4 S**mall (status line) or **S**mall (pull-down menu).

WordPerfect inserts a pair of hidden codes into your document. In this example, WordPerfect inserted a **[SMALL][small]** pair of codes. Your cursor is actually positioned *between* the uppercase "ON" code and the lowercase "off" code. Whatever you type will be in small size until you move the cursor beyond the "off" code.

4. Type *PO Box 86832* on one line and press Enter. Type *Portland, OR 97216* on the next line.

5. To turn off the size code, press Font (Ctrl-F8) and choose **3 N**ormal

or

Choose **N**ormal from the F**o**nt menu.

Note: These menu choices move the cursor past the "off" code. Once you understand this, you can save a few keystrokes by using the right arrow to move the cursor past the "off" code.

6. Press Enter to insert a space between the address and the date.

Depending on your monitor, the text with the new size may or may not look different on-screen. You may have to print or preview the document in order to see the effect.

If you first block the text, you can use these preceding steps to change the size of existing text (see Chapter 7).

Changing justification

One of the ways you control the look of a document is to specify how the text is to be positioned horizontally. For example, whether the text is fully justified (flush left and right) or left-justified (flush left, ragged right), and how tabs, indents, and margin releases are used, all affect the horizontal positioning of the text. WordPerfect comes with the default justification set so that text stretches from the left margin to the right margin. This format, which most books and magazines use, is called *full justification*.

WordPerfect produces full justification by automatically inserting partial spaces between letters (letter spacing) and words (word spacing) until the line fits all the way across a page. Unless you hyphenate the text, this format doesn't look as attractive as left justification. See figure 5.5 for examples of fully justified and left-justified text.

Fully justified for the formal look; left justified (ragged right) for correspondence and a less formal appearance.

This paragraph of text is fully justified, meaning the right margin is even. Spaces are added between words and letters to make the line come out even in the right margin. This paragraph of text is fully justified, meaning the right margin is even. Spaces are added between words and letters to make the line come out even in the right margin. This paragraph of text is fully justified, meaning the right margin is even. Spaces are added between words and letters to make the line come out even in the right margin.

This paragraph of text is left justified, meaning the right margin is "ragged" or uneven. This paragraph of text is left justified, meaning the right margin is "ragged" or uneven. This paragraph of text is left justified, meaning the right margin is "ragged" or uneven. This paragraph of text is left justified, meaning the right margin is "ragged" or uneven. This paragraph of text is left justified, meaning the right margin is "ragged" or uneven.

Fig. 5.5.

Fully justified and left-justified text.

WordPerfect offers four choices for justification:

✳ **Full**. Text is lined up on the left and right margins. Word-Perfect justifies the lines by inserting spaces between letters and words. This is the default setting.

✳ **Left**. Text is lined up only on the left margin. The right margin is not lined up; it is ragged.

✳ **Right**. Text is lined up only on the right margin. The left margin is not lined up; it is ragged.

✳ **Center**. Text is centered.

Right and center justification are not used very often.

Letters, even formal business letters, often look their best when they are left-justified. Do the following to change WordPerfect's justification setting:

1. So that the justification code you insert will affect the entire document, first move the cursor to the beginning of the sample letter (press Home, Home, up arrow).

2. Press Format (Shift-F8) and choose **1 - L**ine

or

Choose **J**ustify from the **L**ayout menu and then choose **L**eft from the pop-out menu.

3. Choose **3 - J**ustification.

4. Choose one of the following: **1 L**eft; **2 C**enter; **3 R**ight; **4 F**ull. (The default factory setting is Full, but someone may have changed your copy to another setting–most likely Left.)

5. Press Exit (F7) to return to the main editing screen.

If you chose **1 L**eft, a **[Just:Left]** hidden code is inserted into your document. All text from that point to the end of the document or until another justification code is encountered will be left-justified. Notice that this is one of the times when using the pull-down menu is more efficient and saves a few keystrokes.

Experiment with other justification settings, by repeating the steps above, to see their effects on-screen. Note: Left and Full justification will look the same on the screen, but will look different in View Document and when you print it (see Chapter 6).

Centering text

Centering text on a typewriter usually means adding up the number of letters in the text, dividing by two, and then backspacing that number of times from the center point. Whew! Sounds like work! With WordPerfect, all that calculating is done automatically for you.

To center the company information in the sample letter, do the following:

1. Move the cursor to the beginning of the word *Sunshine* in the name of the company.

2. Press Center (Shift-F6)

or

Choose **A**lign from the **L**ayout menu; then choose **C**enter from the pop-out menu. (In this case, the function-key approach takes fewer steps than the pull-down menus.)

3. Repeat Steps 1 and 2 for the two address lines.

No more counting and dividing and backspacing and...

With WordPerfect, just press the Center (Shift-F6) key.

```
                         Sunshine Northwest, Inc.
                              PO Box 86832
                            Portland, OR 97216

June 25, 1991

Dear Mr. Jones,

It was a pleasure meeting you yesterday. I was delighted to hear you might be
opening a new health food store. I was also pleased to hear you are
considering featuring our line of nutritional supplements.

As we discussed, here are some discounts we can offer:

Opening Order Second Order Third Order
15% 10% 5%

Here is what the total would be over a period of three months with the
suggested inventory:

First Month 1,000.00
Second Month 550.00
Third Month 400.00
C:\WP51\EASY\FIGS\FIG5-6                        .        Doc 1 Pg 1 Ln 1" Pos 1"
```

Fig. 5.6.

The company information centered between the margins.

Refer to figure 5.6 to see how the information should look on-screen.

The steps you just performed centered the text between margins. You also can center text in a particular place. To do this, first press the space bar or Tab key to move the cursor to where you want text centered; then press Center (Shift-F6). Whenever you press Center (Shift-F6), WordPerfect inserts a **[Center]** code. The code is active until you press Enter.

Notes

Right-aligning text

Sometimes it's appropriate to align text along the right margin. To align date along the right margin, do the following:

1. Move the cursor to the beginning of the date.

2. Press Flush Right (Alt-F6)

or

Choose **A**lign from the **L**ayout menu; then choose **F**lush Right from the pop-out menu. (This is another case in which using the function key takes fewer steps than using the pull-down menus.)

The date text should now align along the right margin (see fig. 5.7). When you press Flush Right (Alt-F6), WordPerfect inserts a **[Flsh Rgt]** code. The code is active until you press Enter.

Want text right aligned? Just press Flush Right (Alt-F6).

```
                    Sunshine Northwest, Inc.
                         PO Box 86832
                      Portland, OR 97216

                                             June 25, 1991

Dear Mr. Jones,

It was a pleasure meeting you yesterday. I was delighted to hear you might be
opening a new health food store. I was also pleased to hear you are
considering featuring our line of nutritional supplements.

As we discussed, here are some discounts we can offer:

Opening Order Second Order Third Order
15% 10% 5%

Here is what the total would be over a period of three months with the
suggested inventory:

First Month 1,000.00
Second Month 550.00
Third Month 400.00

C:\WP51\EASY\FIGS\FIG5-7                      Doc 1 Pg 1 Ln 1" Pos 1"
```

Fig. 5.7.

The date aligned flush right.

5|100 Understanding tabs

Remember, avoid one of the most common mistakes beginners make:

Don't use the spacebar as a substitute for the Tab key.

If you are accustomed to using tabs with a typewriter, you will find that tabs work differently in WordPerfect. Perhaps the most common mistake that beginning WordPerfect users make is to press the space bar instead of using the Tab key. For example, suppose that you want to indent the first line of a paragraph or to create a table that lists columnar data. New users often press the space bar several times to create the indent or the column. On the screen, this looks the same as if you had pressed the Tab key. However, WordPerfect sees things differently. The following explains the difference between typewriter and WordPerfect tabs:

✻ **Typewriter tabs.** With a typewriter, you can either press the Tab key or press the space bar to push the typing element or platen right to the next tab stop. In other words, if you have a tab setting at five spaces, you can get there by pressing either the Tab key once or the space bar five times.

✻ **WordPerfect tabs.** With WordPerfect, when you press the Tab key, a **[Tab]** hidden code is inserted, and the cursor moves to the right and stops at the next tab stop. If instead you press the space bar five times, you have not inserted a hidden code, only five spaces.

Why does it matter how you indent text? The following are two reasons:

✻ **You can change tab settings.** If you later want to change a 1-inch tab to a 1 1/2-inch tab, you can do so by changing the tab settings. If you have just inserted spaces, changing the tab settings will not have any effect.

✻ **Columns may not line up if you use the space bar**

to indent text. If you use a laser printer, most of the fonts you use are probably proportional. If you use spaces to try to align text in a column, proportional type will rarely line up as you expect. Only with monospaced or fixed-pitch fonts will using the space bar work correctly, but then you lose the flexibility of reformatting by just changing tab settings.

Like typewriters, most dot-matrix and daisy-wheel printers use monospaced or fixed-pitch fonts. This means that every character takes up exactly the same amount of space. Most laser printer fonts are proportional, which means that each letter takes up a different amount of space. For example, a w is wider than an i, so the w takes up more space. Proportional fonts are generally more attractive, but monospaced fonts are often useful when columns of figures need to line up. Consult your laser printer manual to see which of your fonts are proportional and which are monospaced. Figure 5.8 shows examples of the use of tabs compared to spaces for alignment.

```
Monospaced font without tabs (aligned using spaces)
    221.23
    891.48
  1,458.22
10,444.87
```

Proportional font without tabs (aligned using spaces)
221.23
891.48
1,458.22
10,444.87

Proportional font with tabs (aligned using tabs)
221.23
891.48
1,458.22
10,444.87

Fig. 5.8.

Monospaced and proportional text aligned by tabs and spaces.

Understanding the Types of Tabs

WordPerfect provides four types of tabs:

✻ **Left**. A left tab is left-justified (text typed from the tab will move right).

✻ **Right**. A right tab is right-justified (text typed from the tab will move left).

❋ **Center**. A center tab is center-justified (text typed will be centered on the tab).

❋ **Decimal**. A decimal tab lines up on a decimal point. This tab is perfect for aligning columns of figures.

Each kind of tab can also have a dot leader. A dot leader is a series of dots that fills the gap between the end of the line of text you typed and the tab stop. Dot leaders are useful for lists like phone directories. Figure 5.9 shows samples of each kind of tab.

Fig. 5.9.

Examples of left, right, center, decimal, and dot leader tabs.

```
Examples of different types of tabs:
                                        this is left aligned
                                        this also is left aligned
                    this is right aligned
              this also is right aligned
                        this is center aligned
                      this also is center aligned
                    this is aligned on a .
              this also is aligned on a .
line one . . . . . . . . . . . . . . . left aligned with a dot leader
line two . . . . . . . . . . . . . . . also left aligned with a dot leader




C:\WP51\EASY\FIGS\FIG5-9                          Doc 1 Pg 1 Ln 1" Pos 1"
```

Changing Tab Settings

WordPerfect comes preset with left tabs set every half-inch. You can change these by doing the following:

1. Press Format (Shift-F8) and choose **1 - Line**

or

Choose **L**ine from the **L**ayout menu.

2. Choose **8 - T**ab Set.

3. You can see your document again (but you can't edit it at this time). At the bottom of the screen is the tab ruler (see fig. 5.10).

Fig. 5.10.

The tab ruler.

```
┌─────────────────────────────────────────────────────────────────┐
│                    Sunshine Northwest, Inc.                       │
│                        PO Box 86832                               │
│                      Portland, OR 97216                           │
│                                                                   │
│                                          June 25, 1991            │
│                                                                   │
│ Dear Mr. Jones,                                                   │
│                                                                   │
│ It was a pleasure meeting you yesterday. I was delighted to hear you might be │
│ opening a new health food store. I was also pleased to hear you are │
│ considering featuring our line of nutritional supplements.        │
│                                                                   │
│ As we discussed, here are some discounts we can offer:            │
│                                                                   │
│ Opening Order Second Order Third Order                            │
│ 15% 10% 5%                                                        │
│                                                                   │
│ Here is what the total would be over a period of three months with the │
│ suggested inventory:                                              │
│ .....L....L....L....L.....L....L.....L...L.....L....L.....L....L....L. │
│     ^      ^      ^      ^       ^      ^      ^      ^           │
│ 0"     +1"    +2"    +3"    +4"      +5"    +6"    +7"            │
│ Delete EOL (clear tabs); Enter Number (set tab); Del (clear tab); │
│ Type; Left; Center; Right; Decimal; .= Dot Leader; Press Exit when done. │
└─────────────────────────────────────────────────────────────────┘
```

Each of the little "L" symbols indicates a left tab. Each of the numbers (like +1" and +2") indicates the distance from the left margin setting. (If there is no plus symbol, the figures are the distance from the left edge of the paper.)

At this point you have several options:

✳ You can **delete all the tab settings** to the right of the blinking cursor by pressing Delete EOL (Ctrl-End).

✳ You can **delete single tabs** either by using the arrow keys to move the cursor to the tab in question and pressing Delete, or by typing a number (which may include a decimal), pressing Enter, and then pressing Delete.

✳ You can **add a new tab** either by using the arrow keys to move the cursor to the tab in question and pressing **L**eft, **C**enter, **R**ight, or **D**ecimal (depending on the type of tab you want to add), or by typing a number (which may include a decimal), pressing Enter, and then pressing the appropriate letter.

✳ You can **change existing tabs** either by using the arrow keys to move the cursor to the tab in question and pressing **L**eft, **C**enter, **R**ight, or **D**ecimal (depending on the type of tab you want to add), or by typing a number (which may include a decimal), pressing Enter, and then pressing the appropriate letter.

✳ You can **insert multiple evenly spaced tabs** by typing

the number where you want tabs to begin, a comma, and the increment and by then pressing Enter. For example, typing *1,.5* inserts half-inch tabs from 1 inch to the right margin.

✻ You can **add a dot leader** to any tab by pressing the period key (.) when the cursor is positioned over an existing tab stop.

4. If you previously inserted tabs into the text that is on-screen, the tabs will dynamically change as you change the tab settings. This feature makes it very easy to line up tabular columns correctly.

5. After you are finished making changes to the tab settings, press Exit (F7) twice to return to the main editing screen.

WordPerfect inserts a **[Tab Set:]** code at the point where the cursor was when you decided to change tabs. All tabs from the hidden code to the end of your document will reflect the new settings unless a new tab code is encountered.

The sample letter contains two places where tabs are needed in order to format information properly. To set up the tabs, do the following:

1. Move the cursor to the word *Second* in the line that begins *Opening*. Press Tab. Now move the cursor to the word *Third* in the same line. Press Tab.

2. Move the cursor to the beginning of *10%* in the next line. Press Tab. Now move the cursor to *5%* and press Tab.

3. Move the cursor to the beginning of the line that begins *Opening*. In the next few steps, you'll be changing the tab settings for the tabs you just inserted.

4. Press Format (Shift-F8) and choose **1 - L**ine

or

Choose **L**ine from the **L**ayout menu.

5. Choose **8 - T**ab Set.

6. Clear all the preset tabs by pressing Del to End of Line (Ctrl-End).

7. Insert left tabs at 2 and 4 inches by typing *2"* and pressing Enter and then typing *4"* and pressing Enter. (You will see the text you tabbed jump to the new positions.)

8. Press Exit (F7) twice to return to the main editing screen.

9. Now you'll set up some decimal tabs. Move the cursor in front of the number *1,000.00* and press Tab. Do the same for the numbers *550.00*, *400.00*, and *1,950.00*. Notice the text move when you tab it. It lines up on the 2-inch tab you set previously. However, numbers look better aligned on a decimal.

10. Move the cursor back to the beginning of the line that starts *First Month*.

11. Press Format (Shift-F8) and choose **1 - L**ine

or

Choose **L**ine from the **L**ayout menu.

12. Choose **8 - T**ab Set.

13. Clear both tabs by pressing Del to End of Line (Ctrl-End).

14. Insert a decimal tab at 3 inches by typing *3"* and pressing Enter; then press D for **D**ecimal to change the left tab into a decimal tab. (You will see the numbers you tabbed jump to their new positions–all aligned on their decimal points.)

15. Press Exit (F7) twice to return to the main editing screen. Refer to figure 5.11 to see how your document should look now.

```
It was a pleasure meeting you yesterday. I was delighted to hear you might be
opening a new health food store. I was also pleased to hear you are
considering featuring our line of nutritional supplements.

As we discussed, here are some discounts we can offer:

Opening Order        Second Order        Third Order
15%                  10%                 5%

Here is what the total would be over a period of three months with the
suggested inventory:

First Month              1,000.00
Second Month               550.00
Third Month                400.00

Total                    1,950.00

We look forward to a warm and mutually beneficial relationship.

Yours truly,


Skye Lininger
C:\WP51\EASY\FIGS\FIG5-11                   Doc 1 Pg 1 Ln 2.22" Pos 1"
```

Fig. 5.11.

New tab settings in effect for the sample letter.

Using indent and margin release

Use the Indent and Margin Release features to control how text paragraphs align on the page.

You can temporarily (one paragraph at a time) change the margins by using either the Indent or the Margin Release feature. The following are the differences between the features:

❋ **Left Indent.** Press ->Indent (F4). Until you press Enter, all text will be indented from the left margin one tab stop. An **[->Indent]** code is inserted. (This kind of indent is used if you want to make one paragraph subordinate to another.)

❋ **Left and Right Indent**. Press ->Indent<- (Shift-F4). Until you press Enter, all text will be indented one tab stop from both the left and right margins. An **[->Indent<-]** code is inserted. (This indent is used when you quote passages that are longer than one or two sentences.)

❋ **Margin Release**. Press ->Margin Release (Shift-Tab). The cursor moves to the left one tab stop. A margin release "releases" the left margin temporarily, just for a single line. The other lines in the paragraph will be lined up on the left margin. A **[<-Mar Rel]** code is inserted. (This feature is used to create special effects like a "hanging paragraph.")

To create a "hanging paragraph" in the sample letter, follow these steps:

1. Position the cursor at the beginning of the paragraph that begins *It was a pleasure*.

2. Press F4 (->Indent). This indents the entire paragraph one tab stop.

3. Press Margin Release (Shift-Tab). This moves the first line of the paragraph back one tab stop.

WordPerfect inserts a **[<-Mar Rel]** hidden code into your text at this point. (In this sample letter, you can either leave this code or delete it.)

This effect, with the paragraph indented and the first line outdented, is called a "hanging indent." See figure 5.12 for examples of indents and the use of the margin release feature.

```
This is a normal paragraph without any indents or tabs effects. The line is
aligned to the left margin.

      This is a paragraph with a Tab inserted at the beginning of paragraph,
creating an indent of the first line, but not the rest of the paragraph.

      This is a paragraph with an ->Indent (F4) pressed at the beginning of the
      paragraph, forcing a left indent of the entire paragraph.

      This is a paragraph with an ->Indent<- (Shift-F4) pressed at the
      beginning of the paragraph, forcing a left and right indent for the
      entire paragraph.

This is a "hanging paragraph" with an ->Indent (F4) pressed and then a
      <- Mar Rel (Shift-Tab) pressed. This creates an indented paragraph with
      an "outdented" first line.
```

`C:\WP51\EASY\FIGS\FIG5-12`   `Doc 1 Pg 1 Ln 1" Pos` 1"

Fig. 5.12.

Examples of indents and margin release.

Changing line spacing

Use the Line Spacing feature to double-space text–don't press the Enter key twice.

Sometimes you will want a document to be double-spaced– for example, if you're an author submitting a manuscript to your publisher. Whatever you do, *don't* press the Enter key twice at the end of each line! Instead, instruct WordPerfect to change the line spacing.

To change the line spacing in the sample letter from 1 to 2, do the following:

1. Move the cursor to the beginning of the letter (press Home, Home, up arrow).

2. Press Format (Shift-F8) and choose **1 - Line**

or

Choose **L**ine from the **L**ayout menu.

3. Choose **6** - **L**ine Spacing.

4. Type *2* and press Enter.

5. Press Exit (F7) to return to the main editing screen.

WordPerfect inserts a **[Ln Spacing]** code. All the text following this code until the end of the document or until another line spacing code is encountered will reflect the new line spacing. If you want the entire document affected, put the code at the beginning of the document (by pressing Home, Home, up arrow).

You can either leave the letter double-spaced, or remove the **[Ln Spacing]** code.

Save the letter for later use in Chapter 6.

Chapter 6: Polishing and printing your document

You've come a long way! In the past three chapters you've learned basic editing and formatting skills and are ready now to produce finished work for the world to see.

The three final steps:
1. proof (use the spell-checker)
2. visualize (use print preview)
3. and print.

This chapter shows you how to spell-check your letter for those pesky misspellings, typographical errors ("typos"), and double words.

You'll learn how you can get a visual preview of your document. Finally, you'll learn how to print your letter or report.

Spell-checking the letter

There's no excuse for misspelled words. Use WordPerfect's spell-checker to catch your spelling errors.

Remember when you typed LETTER.1 in Chapter 3 you included some intentionally misspelled words? Now's the time to correct those.

One of the most useful things about WordPerfect is its Speller. The Speller checks your document for misspellings, suggests correct spellings, and makes corrections for you. If you send out a letter without first spell-checking it, you've only yourself to blame for any spelling errors. The best time to use the spell-checker is after you've finished typing, just before you print your letter.

To use the Speller, do the following:

1. Clear the screen (if necessary) by pressing Exit (F7) and then pressing N in response to Save document? Then press N again in response to Exit WP?

2. Retrieve *LETTER.1*, the practice letter you typed in Chapter 3.

3. Press Spell (Ctrl-F2)

or

Choose Spell from the **T**ools menu.

4. A status-line menu appears at the bottom of your screen. Choose **3 D**ocument (although you can check just a word or page if you like).

5. The screen splits. Your document is in the top window, and the Speller is in the bottom window (similar to the thesaurus, if you recall). The Speller has flagged and highlighted the spelling error *reely* and offers a number of alternative words.

To replace the incorrectly spelled word with the correctly

spelled one, press the letter that appears to the left of the word you want to choose (see fig. 6.1). In this case, press A to replace *reely* with *really*. (It's possible if someone has added words to the spelling dictionary, that "really" won't be choice "A." If that's the case, look for "really" in the list and press the letter that appears next to it.)

Note: If the word you replace was capitalized, WordPerfect automatically capitalizes the correction.

```
Dear Mitch,

It was great you and Jeff could come up for the weekend. We enjoyed your
company. The only problem is the visit was too short.

We reelly liked Jeff's ideas about the liiving room room. After his
explanation, it became clear that the fireplace should be the focal point of
the living room. In order to do that, we now need to look for two new sofas
instead of one!

Our old house finally sold, so we will soon have the money to work with for
                                          Doc 1 Pg 1 Ln 2.22" Pos 1.24"
{    ▲    ▲    ▲    ▲    ▲    ▲    ▲    ▲    ▲    ▲    ▲    }    ▲

    A. really          B. rail           C. railway
    D. rale            E. raleigh        F. rally
    G. rawly           H. rayleigh       I. real
    J. reel            K. reil           L. rela
    M. relay           N. rely           O. rial
    P. riel            Q. rile           R. riley
    S. rill            T. risley         U. riyal
    V. roil            W. role           X. roll
Press Enter for more words

Not Found: 1 Skip Once; 2 Skip; 3 Add; 4 Edit; 5 Look Up; 6 Ignore Numbers: 0
```

6. Next, the Speller flags the word *liiving*. You could press A to replace this with the correct word *living*. However, in this case, let's edit the word instead.

First, select **4** Edit. The Speller window disappears, and the cursor is on *l* in *liiving*. Move the cursor to the letter *i*, delete *i*, and press Exit (F7). Note: You can also use this Edit feature if WordPerfect flags a word but doesn't offer a suggestion for a correct word (often the case with proper names).

7. The next thing the Speller highlights is the double-word sequence *room room*, which begins the second sentence. In this case, the double word is an error, so select **3** Delete 2nd to delete the word *room*.

8. Next, the Speller flags *H7122*. The reason is that *H7122* contains both letters and numbers. WordPerfect stops on words that contain numbers (usually addresses). You can select **6** Ignore Numbers if the flagged word is correct or select **4** Edit if the word is wrong.

9. At the end of the spell-check, the Speller reports to you the number of words in your document. Press any key to return to the main editing screen.

10. Once you've spell-checked your document, remember to save it.

One other note: WordPerfect doesn't know every word in the world, but it's willing to learn. If the Speller flags a word that is correctly spelled (for example, your last name), but WordPerfect doesn't recognize the word, select **3** Add to add the word to a user's dictionary. From then on, WordPerfect will know the word you added. This capability is a useful way to add terms that are specific to your business or to add names of co-workers or customers.

Preparing to print your document

Before you can accurately preview or print your letter or report, you should verify that WordPerfect knows what kind of printer you'll be using.

During the installation process, WordPerfect asks you what printer you plan on using. At that time, WordPerfect automatically installed itself to work with your printer. So, the chances are very good that you already have the correct printer installed and selected.

In some offices, especially if you are on a network, there may be several printers installed. Check with your system administrator or supervisor to find out which printer you should use when printing your documents.

To verify that the correct printer is selected, do this:

1. Look at your printer for the brand and model number.

2. Press Print (Shift-F7)

or

Choose **P**rint from the **F**ile menu.

3. Look to the right of the **S** - **S**elect Printer line (see fig. 6.2) to see which printer has been selected. If this is the same as the printer you will be using, you can skip to the next section.

If your letter won't print, make sure you have selected the correct printer.

If it still won't print, check the power and cable connections.

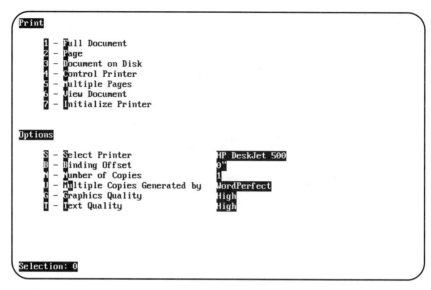

Fig. 6.2.

The Print Options menu.

If the incorrect printer brand or model is selected, you need to select the correct one. The following steps explain how to do this:

1. Choose **S** - **S**elect Printer.

2. At this point, you'll see a screen listing additional printers. If your printer appears in this list, move the cursor bar (using the arrow keys) until your model is chosen; then choose **1** **S**elect and skip to Step 5. If your model isn't on this list, or if this list of additional printers didn't appear, go to Step 3.

3. If your printer still isn't listed, choose **2** **A**dditional Printers. A new list appears. If your printer appears in this list, move the cursor bar (using the arrow keys) until your model is chosen; then choose **1** **S**elect. (If your model isn't on this list, go to the next step.)

Press Enter in response to the `Printer filename` prompt; then press Exit (F7) two times. The cursor should be over the new printer's name (if not, move the cursor by using the arrow keys). Choose **1** **S**elect; then press Exit (F7) to return to the main editing screen.

4. If your printer still isn't listed, or you see a `Printer files not found` message, you'll need to install a printer by using the WordPerfect Install program. An explanation of how to use the Install program to install printer drivers is beyond the scope of a beginner's book. You can ask the person who did the initial installation of WordPerfect to help you, check the WordPerfect manual, refer to an advanced book, or call WordPerfect support.

5. Press Exit (F7) to return to the main editing screen.

Understanding how changing a printer affects your document

If you first type a document and then change the printer selection or the fonts, the composition of the letter may change. What took up three pages with one printer might spill over to four pages with another. A heading that fell at the bottom of a page with one font might be pushed to the top of the next page with another.

WordPerfect handles reformatting chores automatically. Just be aware that when you change printers or fonts, you may change your document. The next section tells you how to preview your document to detect those changes.

Previewing a letter

WordPerfect doesn't show you exactly what your document will look like when it's printed.

The print preview feature gives you a graphical representation of your document.

While WordPerfect does an admirable job of giving you an on-screen of what your letter will look like, it's not the same as seeing a printout. To compensate for this, WordPerfect has a View Document feature that (with most systems that have a graphics card and monitor) allows you to preview your document before you print it. The preview of a document shows a document's position on the page; along with footers and headers, page numbers, and font changes.

If you have not already done so, retrieve the sample LETTER.1 or another file you have created. To preview a document, do the following:

1. Press Print (Shift-F7)

or

Choose **P**rint from the **F**ile menu.

2. Choose **6** - **V**iew Document.

3. A graphical representation of the document is displayed (see fig. 6.3 for an example of a complex document–not LETTER.1). All parts of the document are displayed, including (if present) footers, headers, page numbers, and graphics. Fonts and justification are displayed more accurately.

The status-line menu in the View Document window lets you view the document at **1** 100% (actual size) , **2** 200% (a portion magnified), **3** Full Page (the entire page at once), or **4** Facing Pages (two pages at a time). You cannot edit from the View Document window.

4. Press Exit (F7) to return to the main editing window.

If the document is more than one page, you can move from

one page to the next by pressing the PgUp or PgDn key; you can scroll up and down and side to side by using the arrow keys.

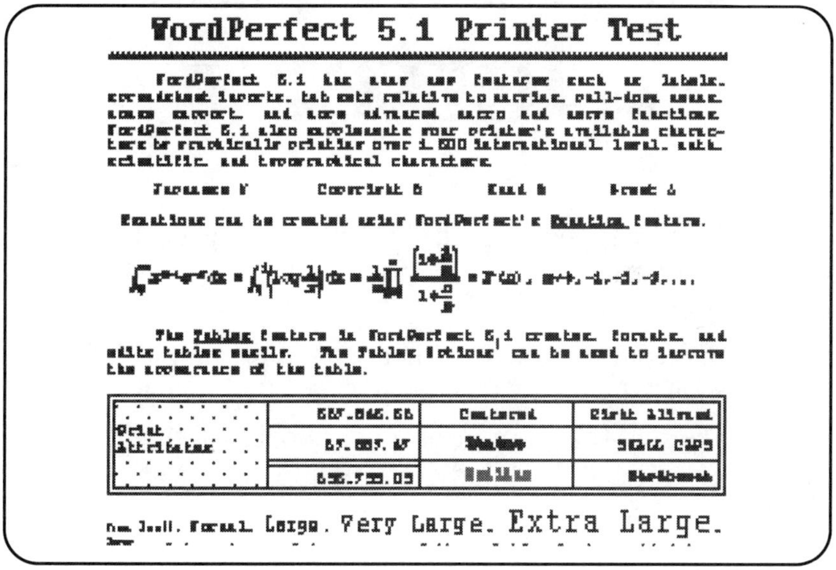

Fig. 6.3.

The View Document window, showing the PRINTER.TST file.

This file demonstrates mathematical equations, graphics, footers, and different font attributes.

Printing the letter

Printing the letter is
as easy as pressing
the Print (Shift-F7) key
and choosing how much
of the document you
want to print.

Once you've typed, edited, spell-checked, saved, and previewed your letter, you're ready to print it. To do so, follow these steps:

1. If necessary, retrieve a document (for example, LETTER.1 or LETTER.2).

2. Make sure that your printer has paper in it, that it is turned on, and that the "ready" or "on-line" light is lit.

3. Press Print (Shift-F7)

or

Choose **P**rint from the **F**ile menu.

4. Choose **1** - **F**ull Document.

You'll see a * `Please wait` * message while WordPerfect sends the document to the printer.

Other options on the Print menu may interest you:

✳ **2** - **P**age. Choosing this option prints only the page where the cursor is.

✳ **5** - **M**ultiple Pages. This option allows you to print selected pages from a longer document. For example, "1-6" specifies the first six pages; "4-5" specifies only pages 4 and 5; "5-" specifies page 5 to the end of the document; and "3,6" specifies pages 3 and 6.

✳ **N** - **N**umber of Copies. This option allows you to print more than one copy at a time.

✳ **G** - **G**raphics Quality and **T** - **T**ext Quality. These options can be set as follows: **1** Do **N**ot Print; **2 D**raft; **3 M**edium; **4 H**igh. Some printers, such as the dot-matrix variety, have a draft mode, which allows for rapid printing. This mode is often useful for the initial proofing of documents.

Chapter 7: Using block and longer document techniques

By this stage, you have learned basic WordPerfect editing and formatting techniques. If your primary use of WordPerfect is for writing short letters, you now know most of what you need to know to do that job.

If you will be writing longer letters, repetitive letters, or reports, this chapter gives you more tools for those kinds of documents.

In this chapter, you will learn how to block text for moving, copying, deleting,

Need techniques for longer letters or reports?

This chapter covers blocks, page numbers, footers, headers, and more.

or modifying. You will also learn how the block technique can help you create "boilerplate" documents.

This chapter will also show you how to handle margins that change from the first page to the second page–a possible problem if you use letterhead stationary.

You will also learn about adding page numbers, footers, and headers to your documents. Finally, you'll be shown how to insert special characters–like foreign letters–into your documents.

This chapter is less tutorial in its orientation than the preceding six. This is because you may or may not be interested in learning all the techniques described. Feel free to skip from one heading to another, looking for useful topics.

Notes

Blocking text

Put away your scissors and glue. If you've ever typed a letter or report and, after reading it over, wished you'd put a sentence or paragraph somewhere else, you'll love WordPerfect's block feature.

Before you can do electronic cutting and pasting, you must learn how to define a block of text.

To WordPerfect, a block is a rectangle of selected text. The blocking procedures involve two steps: The first step is to define the block; the second step is to do something with the block.

Once the block of text has been defined, you can do a number of things to that block:

✻ **Move it.** You can move the block to a new location in your document.

✻ **Copy it.** You can copy the block and put the copy in another location.

✻ **Delete it.** You can delete the block of text.

✻ **Save it.** You can save the block to a new file.

✻ **Change its font attributes.** You can change the appearance or size of the font in a block–including adding or removing bold or underline.

✻ **Position it.** You can center or right-align a block.

To define a block in the sample LETTER.1, do the following:

1. Clear the screen (if necessary) by pressing Exit (F7) and then pressing N in response to Save document? Then press N again in response to Exit WP?

2. Retrieve the document LETTER.1 by pressing Retrieve (Shift-F10). Type *LETTER.1*, and press Enter.

3. Place the cursor at the beginning of the first paragraph (which begins *It was great*).

4. Begin defining the block, using the function keys, the pull-down menus, or the mouse:

Press Block (Alt-F4)

or

Choose **B**lock from the **E**dit menu

or

Position the cursor with the mouse, click the left button, and drag the mouse down and to the right.

You should see the words `Block on` flashing in the left part of the status line.

5. Finish defining the block:

Use the cursor keys (or, if you're using the mouse, click and drag and then release the left button) to move the cursor to the end of the paragraph (which closes with the words *too short*) and select the block. The block is highlighted (see fig. 7.1).

```
June 16, 1991

Dear Mitch,

It was great you and Jeff could come up for the weekend. We enjoyed your company
The only problem is the visit was too short.

We really liked Jeff's ideas about the living room. After his explanation, it be
clear that the fireplace should be the focal point of the living room. In order
that, we now need to look for two new sofas instead of one!

Our old house finally sold, so we will soon have the money to work with for
purchasing new living room furniture.

Would you please ask him if he thinks we should try and get the furniture to mat
the carpet or consider an Oriental rug and then try and match the furniture to i
refresh his memory, we had looked at pattern H7122.

We'll hold you to your promise to visit again before the end of summer.

Yours truly,

Block on                                            Doc 1 Pg 1 Ln 2.17" Pos 4.29"
```

6. If you change your mind and decide you don't want a block of text defined, you can press either Block (Alt-F4) or Cancel (F1) to turn off the block feature.

At this time, press F1 (Cancel) to turn off the block. In the following sections, you'll practice each of the preceding techniques.

Moving blocks of text

Once a block is defined, you can easily move the block. This capability is useful when you want to reorganize the flow of a document or if you want to move part of one document into another document.

To move a block of text, do the following:

1. Define the block you defined in the preceding section.

2. Press Move (Ctrl-F4) and choose **1 B**lock, then choose **1 M**ove

or

Choose **M**ove (Cut) from the **E**dit menu.

When you choose Move, the text disappears from the screen (it is temporarily retained in a WordPerfect text buffer).

```
June 16, 1991

Dear Mitch,

We reelly liked Jeff's ideas about the liiving room room. After his explanation,
became clear that the fireplace should be the focal point of the living room. In
to do that, we now need to look for two new sofas instead of one!

Our old house finally sold, so we will soon have the money to work with for
purchasing new living room furniture.

Would you please ask him if he thinks we should try and get the furniture to mat
the carpet or consider an Oriental rug and then try and match the furniture to i
refresh his memory, we had looked at pattern H7122.

It was great you and Jeff could come up for the weekend. We enjoyed your company
The only problem is the visit was too short.

We'll hold you to your promise to visit again before the end of summer.

Yours truly,

C:\WP51\EASY\FIGS\7-1.TXT                    Doc 1 Pg 1 Ln 1.97" Pos 1"
```

Fig. 7.2.

Letter with block of text moved.

The new location of the block.

3. The `Block on` message is now gone. In its place is the message `Move cursor; press` **Enter** `to retrieve.` Move the cursor (using the cursor keys, keyboard shortcuts, or the mouse) to the end of the paragraph that closes with *H7122*.

4. Press Enter. The text you moved is inserted into the text.

Notice that the text is inserted immediately after the word *H7122* (see fig. 7.2). To form proper paragraphs, press Enter twice more. In addition, the spot you moved the text from now has two extra returns, which can be deleted

Notes

_____

_____

_____

_____

_____

_____

_____

_____

_____

_____

Copying blocks of text

Copying a block of text is identical to moving a block of text–with one exception. When you move a block, the selected text is deleted from its original spot. When you copy a block, the selected text is unaffected and stays in its original spot.

Save the drudgery of retyping the same thing again–learn how to copy blocks of text.

To copy a block of text, do the following:

1. Define the block that reads *visit again before the end of summer.* (See the section "Blocking Text").

2. Press Move (Ctrl-F4) and choose **1 B**lock, then choose **2 C**opy

or

Choose **C**opy from the **E**dit menu.

3. The Block on message is now gone. In its place is the message Move cursor; press **Enter** to retrieve. Move the cursor (using the cursor keys, keyboard shortcuts, or the mouse) to the end of the letter (where it reads *Skye and Jane*).

4. Press Enter. The text you moved is inserted into the text.

5. Press Enter twice more to move the inserted text down two lines.

6. Now, type *P.S. Remember, we want you to.*

The phrase you copied is now part of a new sentence–and you saved time by not having to retype the same words again.

Deleting blocks of text

Need to delete a lot of text at once? Block it first, then delete the block.

Once a block of text is defined (see the section "Blocking Text"), you can delete the entire block in a number of ways:

* Press Delete and then press Y when asked `Delete Block?` (This is the easiest method.)

* Press Move (Ctrl-F4), then choose **1 B**lock, and then choose **3 D**elete.

* Choose **D**elete from the **E**dit menu and press Y when asked `Delete Block?`

Any block you delete can be recovered through WordPerfect's Undelete feature (see Chapter 3).

To delete and undelete a block, do the following:

1. Define the block that reads *P.S.* and ends *end of summer.* (See the section "Blocking Text").

2. Press Delete.

3. Press Y when asked `Delete Block?`

To undelete the block you just deleted, do the following:

1. Press Cancel (F1)

or

Choose **U**ndelete from the **E**dit menu.

You will see the sentence you just deleted appear in highlight on the screen.

2. Press **1 R**estore to undelete the text.

Changing font attributes on blocked text

Once you have defined a block of text, you can change the appearance or size of the block's font. For example, to italicize a selected word in a letter, do the following:

1. Clear the screen (if necessary) by pressing Exit (F7) and then pressing *N* in response to `Save document?` Then press *N* again in response to `Exit WP?`

2. Retrieve LETTER.2.

3. Block the word *pleasure* (see the section "Blocking Text") in the first paragraph.

4. Press Font (Ctrl-F8)

or

Choose the F**o**nt menu.

5. Choose **2 A**ppearance and then select **4 I**talc

or

Choose **A**ppearance from the F**o**nt menu and then select **I**talics from the pop-out menu.

6. The word *pleasure* is now italicized.

If you wanted to either bold or underline the text, you can either choose **B**old or **U**nderline from the **A**ppearance pop-out menu or simply press the Bold (F6) or Underline (F8) key after you have selected text.

Once text is blocked, you can change the text attributes (appearance or size) on the entire block with a single command.

Centering or right-aligning

Once a block has been defined, you can change its justification to either centered or flush right (right-justified). To practice centering an address, do the following:

1. Type the following on three lines:

Sunshine Northwest, Inc.

PO Box 86832

Portland, OR 97286-2724

2. Block the company name and address (see the section "Blocking Text").

3. Press Center (Shift-F6)

or

Choose **A**lign from the **L**ayout menu; then choose **C**enter from the pop-out menu

4. Press Y in response to the [Just:Center]? **N**o (**Y**es) prompt.

The company name and address text you blocked are now centered between the left and right margins.

To right-align the text, change Steps 3 and 4 as follows:

3. Press Flush Right (Alt-F6)

or

Choose **A**lign from the **L**ayout menu; then choose **F**lush Right from the pop-out menu

4. Press Y in response to the [Just:Right]? **N**o (**Y**es) prompt.

The company name and address text you blocked are now flush right, or right-justified, on the right margin.

Learning about "boilerplate" letters

One of the niftiest time-savers available to WordPerfect users is the ability to reuse text you've typed before. If you send out letters that contain some of the same paragraphs, you may prefer not to have to retype them over and over. Paragraphs used again and again are termed *boilerplate*. Using a combination of the block, save, and retrieve features, you will never have to retype a boilerplate paragraph again.

Although what follows is just sample text, if you perform the steps, you'll learn the basic concept behind assembling a boilerplate letter. Do the following to practice creating a boilerplate letter:

1. Clear the screen (if necessary) by pressing Exit (F7) and then pressing *N* in response to `Save document?` Then press *N* again in response to `Exit WP?`

2. Type the text in LETTER.3 (see fig. 7.3).

3. Save the document as LETTER.3.

Saving a block to a file

To save a block of text to a file that can be used again, do the following:

1. Using the text you just typed in LETTER.3, block the text that begins with *It was nice meeting you* and ends with *health foods' section.* (See the section "Blocking Text.")

2. Press Save (F10)

or

> Once you learn the secrets of "boilerplate text," you won't have to retype stock paragraphs ever again.

It was nice meeting you last week. I appreciate the time you were able to spend talking about our products. It was especially exciting to know you're interested in adding some of our products to (store) health foods' section.

I've had the company forward to you sample bottles of (number) items. I selected these particular items because they are among our proven best sellers. The number of items I'm suggesting will fill (number) feet of shelf space. One reason for sending all the samples is so you can verify what will fit on the shelf.

We have UPC's on the labels for half the items. We will place UPC stickers on the bottle for the items that do not yet have printed UPC's. I've been told by our label purchaser that the remainder of these items will be coded within five months at the latest. I've spoken to our plant manager, and he has promised to get to work immediately on the items you're interested in, so I think that within months we'll have UPC's in place on all the items you will carry.

I look forward to working with you in providing quality products to your customers, in providing educational presentations to your staff, and in creating literature that you can use in educating your customers and staff. I look forward to hearing from you after you have had a chance to review the things I've sent.

Yours truly,

Skye Lininger, D.C.
Vice President, Sales

Fig. 7.3.

The sample LETTER.3.

Choose **S**ave from the **F**ile menu.

3. On the status line, you'll see the prompt `Block name:`. Type *ONE.BP* and press Enter. That block has now been copied to the disk and is saved in the file called ONE.BP.

(The file name extension BP stands for "boilerplate," but you can use any extension you want depending on what helps you remember what's in the file.)

Repeat steps 1-4 to block and save the second paragraph as TWO.BP, the third as THREE.BP, and so on. Save the entire signature block as SIG.BP. (See fig. 7.4.)

Assembling a letter from boilerplate

To assemble a letter from your BP (boilerplate), do the following steps:

1. Clear the screen by pressing Exit (F7). Press N at the `Save document?` prompt; then press N at the `Exit WP?` prompt.

2. Press Retrieve (Shift-F10)

or

Choose **R**etrieve from the **F**ile menu.

3. Type *ONE.BP* and press Enter. (Remember, you can use List Files [F5] at this point if you prefer. See Chapter 3.)

4. Repeat Step 5, substituting the other file names (TWO.BP and so on). As you do this, you will see the boilerplate letter developing.

5. Finally, retrieve the SIG.BP file. (You may want to create your own signature block that you can quickly incorporate into your own letters. You have only to type your name and address one more time before letting WordPerfect do it for you in the future!)

If you find yourself typing the same thing over and over again, consider getting into the habit of saving those oft-used paragraphs or pages of text for boilerplate assembly.

In the example just given, several spots included fill-ins (for example, for a store name or a number). Filling in these blanks helps you customize and personalize these boilerplate paragraphs further. Using the concepts presented in this section, you can increase your efficiency and avoid extra or redundant work.

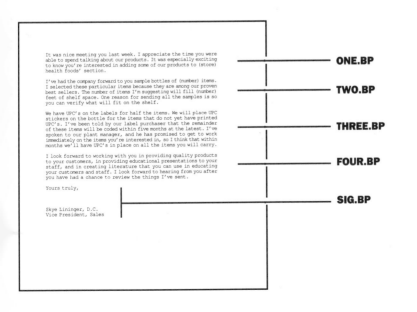

Fig. 7.4

Schematic of LETTER.3 showing boilerplate paragraphs.

Setting margins for second sheets

If you use stationery, this section shows you how to have different margins for the second page.

Another potential problem if you write longer letters is you may have different margins for the first page compared to the following pages. For example, many times, pre-printed letterhead or stationery is used only for the first page of a letter. If a letter is more than one page long, following pages are printed on what is called "second sheet," or paper without anything pre-printed on it. When you change top and bottom or left and right margins to accommodate pre-printed paper, those margin changes remain in place for the entire letter.

For example, if you have a 2 1/2-inch logo, you want the letter to begin printing about 3 inches from the top of the paper. A natural and logical thing to do is change the top margin to 3 inches. But this margin change affects not only the first page of your letter but also the margin for all the pages that follow.

If the second and following pages of your letter or report have margins different from the first sheet's, you need to know how to specify one set of margins for the first page of your letter and another set of margins for the rest of the letter. There are two solutions to this problem:

✱ After typing your letter, go to the top of the second page and change the margins. Because changing the margins inserts a hidden code, the rest of the document is affected from that point onward. In other words, a new margin code at the top of the second page changes the rest of the pages in your letter.

✻ If your left and right margins will be the same on both the first and following pages of your letter, you don't need to change those margins. Instead of changing the top margin on the first page to accommodate pre-printed letterhead or stationary, use WordPerfect's Advance feature (see Chapter 4).

Notes

_____

_____

_____

_____

_____

_____

_____

_____

_____

_____

_____

_____

Making text adjustments

Once you have printed out a full page of text, do a quick measurement of the margins with a ruler. If you haven't changed the margins from the default settings, you should have a 1-inch margin all around (top, bottom, left, and right).

If you have changed the margins or used the Advance feature, the margins should correspond to what you entered. If the margins are all correct, you can skip over the rest of this section. If there is a discrepancy, it is probably due to your printer, and you will need to make an adjustment.

For certain printers (usually dot-matrix) whose print head doesn't touch the top of the physical piece of paper, WordPerfect begins calculating the "advance to line" from where the print head is. For example, if the print head rests 1 inch from the top of the page, then when you set a top margin of 1 inch, WordPerfect doesn't take into account the 1 inch that is above the print head; WordPerfect actually gives you a 2-inch margin. Or if you set "advance to line" to 3 inches, WordPerfect adds 1 inch to the 3 inches and actually prints the first line 4 inches below the top of the page.

You can compensate for this problem by using the Text Adjustment feature. Do the following:

1. Press Format (Shift-F8) and choose **2 - P**age.

or

Choose **P**age from the **L**ayout pull-down menu.

2. Choose **7** - Paper **S**ize/Type.

3. Choose **5 E**dit.

4. Choose **9** - **T**ext Adjustment.

5. Make changes based on the amount of margin discrepancy. For example, if the top margin is 2 inches instead of 1 inch, you need to adjust up by 1 inch. In that case, choose **1 Up**, type *1*", and press Enter. Make other adjustments as necessary.

6. Press F7 (F7) three times to return to your document.

Now reprint your page to verify that the margins are correct. You need only enter the Text Adjustment one time. WordPerfect remembers the change and will automatically calculate the adjustment in the future.

Notes

Numbering pages

Use WordPerfect's page numbering capability to automatically number the pages of your document.

If you have more than one page of text, you may want to number the pages. To number pages, do the following:

1. Clear the screen by pressing Exit (F7). Press N at the `Save document?` prompt; then press N at the `Exit WP?` prompt.

2. Retrieve LETTER.1 (this example uses only a one-page document, but the information carries over for multi-page letters or reports).

3. If necessary, move the cursor to the top of the document (press Home, Home, up arrow).

4. Press Format (Shift-F8) and choose **2** - **P**age

or

Choose **P**age from the **L**ayout menu.

Fig. 7.5.

The Page Number Position menu.

```
Format: Page Number Position


     Every Page                    Alternating Pages
   ┌─────────────┐         ┌─────────────┐ ┌─────────────┐
   │ 1   2   3   │         │ 4           │ │           4 │
   │             │         │             │ │             │
   │             │         │ Even        │ │        Odd  │
   │             │         │             │ │             │
   │ 5   6   7   │         │ 8           │ │           8 │
   └─────────────┘         └─────────────┘ └─────────────┘


        9 - No Page Numbers




Selection: 0
```

5. Choose **6** - Page **N**umbering.

6. Choose **4** - Page Number **P**osition

7. You have eight choices for where you want WordPerfect to place the page number (see fig. 7.5). For this example, select **6** (Bottom Center).

The `Every Page` options will print the page number in the same place on every page.

The `Alternating Pages` choices will alternate where the page numbers go, depending on whether the page number is even or odd. For example, choice 8 may be useful for reports in which you want the page number always to appear on the outside edge.

8. Press Exit (F7) to return to the main editing screen.

WordPerfect inserts a **[Pg Numbering]** code into the document. WordPerfect doesn't display the page numbers on-screen. You will see them, however, when you preview or print the document.

Creating footers and headers

Longer letters or reports often require footers or headers for additional information –including to/from information, subject, and page numbers.

Sometimes you'll want the same information–such as the report's title, the document's date, or the name of the author–to appear at the top or bottom of each page. Identical, repeating information like this is called a *header* when it appears at the top of a page and is called a *footer* when it appears at the bottom of a page.

To create a footer that appears on every page, do the following:

1. Clear the screen by pressing Exit (F7). Press N at the `Save document?` prompt; then press N at the `Exit WP?` prompt.

2. Retrieve LETTER.1.

3. If necessary, go to the beginning of the document (press Home, Home, up arrow).

4. Press Format (Shift-F8) and choose **2 - P**age

or

Choose **P**age from the **L**ayout menu.

5. Choose **4 - F**ooters.

6. Choose **1** Footer **A**.

7. Choose **2** Every **P**age.

8. You are now in the Footer A editing screen. Type the following:

Skye Lininger, Page ^B.

When the letter is printed, the ^B will be replaced by the current page number. You create the ^B by pressing Ctrl-B.

9. Press Exit (F7) twice to return to the main editing screen.

WordPerfect inserts a **[Footer]** code into the document.

The following are some ideas for using footers and headers:

✱ Experiment with centering the footer or header or with making it flush right.

✱ You can make the footer or header several lines long.

✱ You can choose to have the footer or header appear only on odd or even pages (see Step 7.)

✱ You can have two headers or footers (A and B–see Step 5), using one for odd pages and another for even pages.

Editing a footer or header

Once you have created a footer or header, you may want to change its text. To edit the footer you created in the preceding section, do the following:

1. Press Format (Shift-F8) and choose **2 - P**age

or

Choose **P**age from the **L**ayout menu.

2. Choose **4 - F**ooters.

3. Choose **1** Footer **A**.

4. Choose **5 E**dit.

5. You are now in the Footer A editing screen. The following text should be there: *Skye Lininger, Page ^B.*

6. Insert the word *Number* between the word *Page* and the ^B.

7. Press Exit (F7) twice to return to the main editing screen.

Turning off a footer, header, or page number

If you don't want a footer, header, or page number to appear on a particular page of a document (as on page 1), do the following:

1. Press Format (Shift-F8) and choose **2** - **P**age

or

Choose **P**age from the **L**ayout menu.

2. Choose **8** - **Su**ppress (this page only).

3. Choose one of the eight options presented. Choices 3 through 8 require you to press Y (for Yes) to confirm the choice.

4. Press Exit (F7) to return to the main editing screen.

WordPerfect inserts a **[Suppress]** code into the document. The footer, header, or page number won't print on the page where the code appears. This code doesn't affect other pages of the document.

Notes

_____

_____

_____

_____

_____

_____

_____

_____

_____

Inserting special characters

If you type letters in languages other than English, or you need less frequently used typographical symbols (like the registered trademark or the copyright symbol), you'll be impressed by the flexibility of WordPerfect. Altogether, WordPerfect can print more than 1,500 different characters.

Some of the characters include letters with diacritical marks (useful for Spanish and French words); mathematical and scientific symbols; Greek, Hebrew, Cyrillic, Hiragana and Katakana alphabets.

Whether all characters in the WordPerfect character set will print depends on the type of printer you have and the font. Most dot-matrix and laser printers will print all the characters. Not all fonts have all 1,500 characters available.

To see which special characters are available, you can either refer to your WordPerfect manual or print out the file CHARACTR.DOC that came with your copy of WordPerfect. The file should be located in the WP51 directory.

Not all special characters will appear accurately on-screen (sometimes only a small black square is shown). However, they will appear when you preview or print your document.

To insert a special character, do the following:

1. To find the character you want, refer to your WordPerfect manual or the CHARACTR.DOC file that you printed out. For example, if you want to enter the symbol for the British

Need a diacritical mark (â, é, or ñ) over a letter in a foreign word?

Require a copyright (©) or trademark (™ or ®) symbol?

Use WordPerfect's special character set.

pound (£), look in character set 4 (Typographic Symbols) and see character number 11. You'll find that the number for the British pound is "4,11."

2. Press Compose (Ctrl-V)

or

Choose Characters from the Font menu.

3. At the Key = prompt on the status line, type *4,11*.

4. Press Enter.

5. The symbol for the British pound should appear on-screen (with some monitors or printers, you may see only a small black box).

If you place the cursor on the British pound symbol and look in Reveal Codes, you'll see that WordPerfect has inserted the code **[£ :4,11]**.

Summary

You're now at the end of this book. As promised, you've not had to trudge through a thousand pages to learn how to use WordPerfect to accomplish the basic work of writing, editing, and printing a letter or short document.

Congratulations!

By getting to this point, you've learned the basics of WordPerfect and are able to create letters and reports with the world's most popular word processor.

Once you master the techniques in this book, you may want to move on to more advanced texts. There are a number of excellent books on WordPerfect that range from complete compendiums to specialized books. Peachpit Press publishes several other books about Word-Perfect—like *Desktop Publishing in Style*—that you may be interested in.

Good luck with your writing and enjoyment of the power and ease of WordPerfect.

Notes

_____

_____

_____

_____

_____

_____

_____

_____

_____

_____

_____

_____

_____

_____

_____

_____

_____

_____

Appendix A: Understanding WordPerfect's defaults

The subject of defaults and overrides is a bit tricky, so don't be concerned if you need to read over this appendix more than once. Some of this information is fairly advanced, but you need to understand these concepts if you're to get the most out of WordPerfect. There are several levels of defaults and overrides:

✻ **Setup Initial Codes.** WordPerfect comes with all the defaults preset. Every time you start WordPerfect, these defaults are activated. Any changes you make to the initial codes from Setup's Initial Settings (accessed through Shift-F1 or from the File menu) affect

The factory settings in WordPerfect are called "defaults."

This appendix shows you how to change those defaults to customize WordPerfect.

WordPerfect's Setup Initial Codes and are permanent until you change them again at a later date. These settings, once changed, affect all new documents you create.

✻ **Document Initial Codes.** Each time you create a new document, the default settings in effect at the time the document is created are stored with the document. This means that even if you have changed the Setup Initial Codes, documents created with other defaults in place won't have their defaults altered. (This arrangement protects you from accidentally having an older document automatically reformat when you don't want it to.) In any given document, you can override the *Setup* Initial Codes by changing *Document* Initial Codes from the Format menu (accessed by pressing Shift-F8 or choosing **D**ocument from the **L**ayout menu). Changes here won't affect any document other than the one you are currently editing.

✻ **Hidden formatting codes.** WordPerfect gives you complete control over virtually every aspect of your document. If you want to override initial codes temporarily (at either the setup or the document level), you can insert formatting codes (called *hidden codes*—see Chapter 2 for more information). You will also use hidden codes for (among other things) temporary font, justification, tab, and margin changes.

✻ **Styles.** If you find yourself repeatedly using specific formatting, you will want to learn about WordPerfect's Style feature. For example, if you work in a law office or a movie studio and have specific formatting requirements for legal documents or scripts, you can save time by storing a group of hidden codes in what is called a *style*. Then, whenever you want to apply the format to a paragraph or document, you can turn the style on. A full discussion of styles is too complex for this book. If you want to learn about styles, you can review the WordPerfect manual or read an advanced WordPerfect book.

The distinctions among Setup, Document, Hidden Codes, and Styles are often confusing to new WordPerfect users. Usually you'll modify setup or document defaults when you need to change the formatting for entire documents. More often, you'll be inserting hidden codes to affect formatting at the local level.

What are some of WordPerfect's defaults?

WordPerfect's defaults fall into several basic categories. Most of these defaults are controlled from Setup (Shift-F1), and many of these topics are too advanced for this book. If you need to know more about defaults, refer to the WordPerfect manual or an advanced book about WordPerfect. The following briefly discusses WordPerfect's default categories:

From your mouse to your display, WordPerfect has factory default settings.

✻ **Mouse.** The mouse defaults tell WordPerfect what kind of mouse you have. They also let the program know how the mouse is connected to the computer and whether you will operate the mouse with your left hand. If you don't have a mouse, don't worry about these defaults. If you have a mouse, look at the documentation that came with it to see what some of these settings should be.

✻ **Display.** The display defaults tell WordPerfect what kind of monitor your computer has. You also can tell WordPerfect how you want various fonts to display on-screen and which options you prefer with the pull-down menus (see Chapter 2).

✻ **Environment.** These defaults control the WordPerfect working environment. For example, you can control backup and beep options, cursor speed, hyphenation, and how you want things measured (in inches or centimeters, for example), among other things.

✳ **Initial settings.** These settings control some basic formatting defaults. Through initial settings, you set initial codes. You also can change settings concerning merge codes, date format, equations, repeat value (the number you see when you press the Esc key), and print options.

✳ **Keyboard layout.** You can use the keyboard layout to change how various keys are interpreted by WordPerfect. For example, you can set up Alt-12 to switch between documents.

✳ **Location of files.** These settings tell WordPerfect which directories to look in for various files. It's not a good idea to have all your files in the same WP51 directory, because such an arrangement makes files hard to locate. By changing the file location settings, you can place various files in different subdirectories. The most important setting to think about changing is the one for document location–the place where WordPerfect stores and looks for documents you create.

✳ **Printer.** WordPerfect has almost all the choices for printers available from Print (accessed through Shift-F7 or by choosing Print from the **F**ile menu). Normally, your printer should have been set up when you installed WordPerfect. Chapter 6 shows you how to change a printer and print a document.

✳ **Paper size, type, and labels.** WordPerfect allows for virtually any size and kind of paper your printer can handle. You access these choices by pressing Format (Shift-F8) and then choosing 2 - **P**age (or choosing **P**age from the **L**ayout menu).

Changing Setup Initial Codes

This section explains how to change Setup Initial Codes defaults, but you won't want to do that until you understand which defaults you might want to change. If you find yourself continually inserting the same hidden formatting codes at the beginning of a document, you'll want to eventually just make them the default setting. Until you know that you want to do that, just skim over this information so that you'll know where to find it when you need it.

You control these defaults by changing the Initial Codes from the Setup menu by doing the following:

1. Press Setup (Shift-F1) and choose **4** - **I**nitial Settings

or

Choose Se**t**up from the **F**ile menu; then choose **I**nitial Settings from the pop-out menu.

2. Choose **5** - Initial **C**odes.

3. The screen splits into two halves. The bottom half of the screen displays any hidden codes (see fig. A.1). Insert or delete any formatting codes you want.

Modify Setup Initial Codes to change defaults for all new documents you create.

A| 150

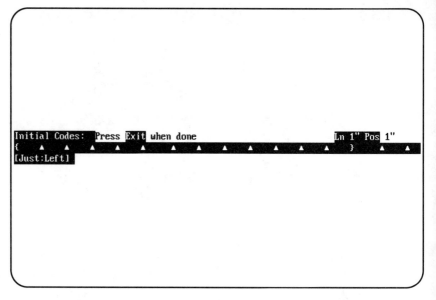

**The hidden codes screen
with a [Just:Left] code.**

4. Press Exit (F7) twice to return to the main editing screen.

Some people have several Initial Codes; others have just one or two.

Remember, Setup Initial Codes affect only new documents. To change document defaults for existing documents, you'll need to change the Format Initial Codes.

Changing Document Initial Codes

You control Document Initial Codes defaults by changing the Initial Codes from the Format menu. To change these settings, do the following:

1. Press Format (Shift-F8) and choose **3 - D**ocument

or

Choose **D**ocument from the **L**ayout menu.

2. Choose **2** - Initial **C**odes.

3. The screen splits into two halves. The bottom half of the screen displays any hidden codes. (Any codes you inserted in the Setup Hidden Codes screen will be included here.) Insert or delete any formatting codes you want.

4. Press Exit (F7) twice to return to the main editing screen.

Remember, Document Initial Codes changes affect only the document you are working on–and should really be used just to override Setup Initial Codes defaults. If you want to affect all new documents, you'll need to modify the Setup Initial Codes.

Modify Document Initial Codes to change default settings for the document that you're currently working on.

A|152

Notes